NOT A GENUINE BLACK MAN

NOT A GENUINE **BLACK** MAN

Or, How I Claimed My Piece of Ground

in the Lily-White Suburbs

BRIAN COPELAND

HYPERION

NEW YORK

Note to Reader: Some of the names and identifying characteristics of persons written about in this book have been changed to protect their identities. Also, the time line for some of the events described in the book has been altered in order to present a more unified story. All other descriptions of persons, places, and events are from the author's recollections and in some instances may have also been confirmed by historical research undertaken by the author.

Library of Congress Cataloging-in-Publication Data

Copeland, Brian.
    Not a genuine black man, or, How I claimed my piece of ground in the lily-white suburbs / Brian Copeland.—1st ed.
        p. cm.
    ISBN 1-4013-0233-5
    1. Copeland, Brian. 2. Comedians—United States—Biography. 3. African American comedians—Biography. I. Title: Note a genuine black man. II. Title: How I claimed my piece of ground in the lily-white suburbs. III. Title.
PN2287.C616A3 2006
792.702'8092—dc22
[B]   2006041241

Hyperion books are available for special promotions and premiums. For details contact Michael Rentas, Assistant Director, Inventory Operations, Hyperion, 77 West 66th Street, 12th floor, New York, New York 10023, or call 212-456-0133.

Design by Jonathan Lippincott

FIRST EDITION

10   9   8   7   6   5   4   3   2   1

For Adam, Carolyn, Casey, and Kris—
may you always be proud of where you came from

"The consistent factor that Great men of the twentieth century shared was a mother who loved them unconditionally, gave them the freedom to express their promise and made them believe that it was possible to achieve anything."

—Mamie Till-Mobley
Mother of Emmett Till

Contents

"YOU Are Not a Genuine Black Man!"

It has often been said that comedians deal with pain through humor. We laugh so we don't have to cry. I know that's true for me. I have spent much of my life laughing to keep the tears at bay, trying to stay one step ahead of the sadness and the despair. Like most of my colleagues in the game that we call stand-up comedy, I've used levity to fuel my flight. It's the motor that helps me to escape the things I can't handle. So when I got a letter that especially upset me one day, I responded with my natural instincts. Rather than truly deal with it, I wrote and performed the following routine:

> Although I'm a stand-up comic by trade, I also do a radio show for a talk station in San Francisco. I'd been out on the road for a couple of weeks doing comedy, and when I got back into the station, I had all this mail piled up. In talk radio, mail generally comes to you from two sources: old ladies and whack jobs. That's it. Old ladies and kooks. Nobody else writes you. That's the downside. The upside is that it makes the mail easy to sort.
>
> So, I'm going through the pile. Old lady. Old lady. Death threat. Old lady. Death threat. Ooh, here's a good one. Death threat from an old lady.

Then, I come across one that's typed . . . I mean typed on an actual typewriter. What antique shop did that one come from? Where do you find ribbon for a typewriter in the twenty-first century? Do you walk into Office Depot?

"Do you have any typewriter ribbon?"

"As a matter of fact we do. Right over there next to the buggy whips. No, over there across from the whale-oil lamps. By the icebox."

So, I look at this envelope. Addressed to me. Local postmark. No return address. I open it, taking out a single, unsigned typewritten sheet that reads:

"As an African American, I am disgusted every time I hear your voice because YOU are not a genuine black man!"

I'm *not* a genuine black man. I am *not* a genuine black man?

Okay, I'll be honest. I'd heard that one before. Actually, people have said that to me a lot throughout my life. Generally, when I hear it I like to give the intellectual response:

"FUCK YOU!!!"

I then grab myself and ask, "Is this black enough for your ass?"

Not a genuine black man. Why do people say that to me? Is it how I talk? Is it how I dress? Is it how my machine is set to TiVo *Frasier*?

I don't even know what that means. If you're talking about pigment, you can tell by looking at me that I am clearly black. But if you're talking about some cultural delineation, I don't know. I don't talk ghetto. When I hear the word "ax," I think of it as a noun. It's not a verb.

"I'm gonna go 'ax' my mother."

Who are you? Lizzie Borden?

I'm Catholic. Is that "black"? I was an altar boy for five years.

Apparently, one of the "lucky" ones.

True story: Not too long ago a priest I served mass with as a child was arrested for abusing altar boys during the time that I was serving mass with him! My only question is: What was wrong with me? Wasn't I cute? What, Father only wanted the white altar boys? What kind of racist bullshit is that? At the very least it would've been nice to be asked. Or axed.

I like old Motown; that's black. But I also like the Beach Boys. That isn't.

I don't believe blacks should be paid reparations for slavery, but if they send me the check, I'll cash it. I'm confused, I'm not crazy.

I can't swim. That's black. But I can't play basketball, either. I'm not even sure that's male.

I like chitlins. But I call them chitterlings. That's what they're called. Read the bucket. Chitterlings. To me that always sounded like a family name.

"The Chitterlings are coming over for dinner this evening."

"Aw man, those nasty-ass people stink up the house every time they come over here."

I love watermelon, but I won't buy one at the store. I refuse. I'm not going to shuffle up to the clerk at Safeway with a big green melon under my arm. Rochester I ain't!

"Hellooo, Mr. Benny. I done gots us the dessert!"

Not me. Sorry.

I don't talk back to the screen at the movie theater. Now that is definitely a black phenomenon. Black people, do not even begin to delude yourselves into thinking that you have no idea what I'm talking about.

"Oh, don't go in there! He hidin' up in there! He got a gun in there. He behind the door!"

HE CAN'T HEAR YOU!!! I just spent ten bucks to get in and sixty-seven dollars for popcorn. SHUT THE HELL UP!

I'm a Democrat. That's black. I've never understood black Republicans. To me, a black in the Republican Party is like a deer joining the National Rifle Association.

"Yes I'm a deer, but I'm not one of those deer!"

Cops think I'm black. Especially in the suburbs.

Cab drivers think I'm black. Even the ones with turbans, and that's what I don't understand. Now let me get this straight. You look like you just crawled out of a cave in Afghanistan with a bomb strapped to your torso, and you're afraid to pick my ass up?

Okay, he's just profiling me like I'm profiling him. Since 9/11 we're all profiling each other, consciously or unconsciously. We're all doing it. I called the FBI because my daughter got out of the shower with a towel on her head. It's okay. They cleared her. Eventually.

Not a genuine black man. What does that mean? If you think about it, throughout American history, it has always been the racists who determine what the racial categories are. For example the Irish weren't considered white when they first came to America. Then apparently white people had a meeting. They all huddled in a circle, arms linked and debated.

"What do you think? Yeah? Okay then. O'Leary, you're in. McDonald, too. What's that? He's Scottish?? No. No sheep fuckers. Just O'Leary."

Are black people doing this now, too? Did this letter come to me from some Soul Patrol Commission on Blackness? Are they reviewing applications?

"Let's see. Bryant Gumbel? He's out. Kobe raped a white woman . . . so she claims. He's persecuted. He can stay. Michael Jackson? We ain't ever heard of him. O.J.? White people can have him, but dead or alive, we're keepin' Johnnie Cochran!"

Who decides this stuff?

Racial identity has always been a confusing issue for me. It was a changing, mutable concept as far back as I can remember. As a very young child, I remember being colored. Whenever we'd run into other dark-skinned people, Grandma would refer to them as colored.

"Go over there and ask that colored man where the canned peaches are," she'd say to me at the grocery store.

Then, one day when I was about four or five, I said something in front of my mother about being colored.

"Don't say that! You're black. You're black. I'm black. We're a black family. We're black."

This was the late '60s and she bought one of those mass-produced paintings with the black woman wearing the huge afro and hoop earrings, cradling a little huge-afro-wearing boy to her breast, with the caption BLACK IS BEAUTIFUL. So, for a long time, I was black.

Then, one day at school, we were given some government paper that had race boxes that the class was to check. I was six years old and confused because no place on this form was the word "black." I asked the teacher, who, incidentally, was white, what to do.

"You're a Negro," she told me. "Check the box that says 'Negro.'"

I thought I was black, but okay, I'll check Negro. So, I was a Negro. Or at least I was for a few weeks until I said something about Negroes in front of my mother.

"I thought I told you that you were black," she shrieked.

"But the paper with the boxes said I'm a Negro."

"Well the paper's wrong!"

So, I was black again. I was black for a very long time, until one day in high school, somebody said to me, "Don't say black. Charcoal is black. Do you look like charcoal? Asphalt is black. Are you the same color as asphalt?"

"No, I guess not," I answered, after giving it some thought.

"You are a person of color."

"A person of color?" I asked, more confused than ever.

"Yes," came the response. "A person of color."

"Well what's the difference between a 'person of color' and a 'colored person'?"

"I don't know. They're just different, that's all."

So, fine, I was a "person of color". . . for a while. Until college, when this girl who was militantly active in the politics and issues of people of African descent jumped all over me for using the phrase.

"A person of color?" she said. "What are you, desegregating buses? Marching from Selma to Montgomery?

You are African American. Your ancestors came from
Africa. Had they come from Italy, you'd be Italian
American. If they were from Ireland, you'd be Irish
American. They were from Africa; that makes you
African American."

"All right," I thought driving home from school
that day. "I finally have it. This makes sense. I'm
African American."

Then, I made a lane change and accidentally cut off
a white motorist. He rolled down his window and
screamed, "Nigger!"

It's confusing. I don't understand why the NAACP
is still called the N double-A C P. The National Association for the Advancement of Colored People. We can
at least agree that we haven't been colored since the
'60s. It should probably be the National Association for
the Advancement of African-American People. The N
triple-A P. That way, we not only get equality, we get
road service.

Whatever the answer is, I've always been a person
who believes in personal responsibility. It starts with
me. It ends with me. Therefore, any confusion I have
about race, any misunderstanding I have about ethnic-
ity, any confusion I have about blackness . . . is my
mother's fault.

The routine was very successful. I performed it to roars of
(sometimes nervous) laughter across America, as the opening
act for Smokey Robinson. The piece was well received in ven-
ues from Constitution Hall in Washington D.C. to the Fox
Theater in St. Louis to the Universal Amphitheater in Holly-
wood. My "funny mask" had won the day again. Behind most

of our masks, however, is a truth that is hidden for a specific reason. Often, we don't even know what that truth is. I wasn't ready to deal with my truths, but ready or not, they started to bubble to the surface. Once that began to happen, try as I might, I couldn't get the toothpaste to go back into the tube.

I had to face a truth that started with my mother.

PART 1

CHAPTER 1

Double Negatives

D id you ever have a day that, even though you didn't know it at the time, would change the course of your entire life? I had a day like that. Images from that day play out in my head like scenes in a movie. Images of hands. Little hands. My eight-year-old hands reaching across a square glass coffee table toward a deck of blue Bicycle playing cards. You know the ones—with the squiggly hieroglyphics and the three circles in the middle with the naked, chubby angel on a bike riding toward you.

Suddenly, another hand darts into the picture. A smaller hand. An annoying little hand with chipped red nail polish and a thumb flattened from years of sucking. My sister, Tracie. She's six.

"It's *my* deal!" she shouted in her lisping, high-pitched voice.

You know, it's been thirty years and I still don't know what her deal is. We were in our house, in the Bay Area town of Hayward, California, playing rummy—or as my family calls it, five hundred. I was glad that we were playing. It had been a rough day. I needed the distraction.

"I said, it's *my* deal!!" she ranted.

"No, it's *my* deal!" I shouted right back at her.

"Mom!"

My younger sisters, Delisa, age four, and Tonya, two, looked up from their Barbie camper. Too young and disinterested to play cards, they were taking Barbie and one of my G.I. Joes on a date. The shrieking of the word, "'Mom," broke the magic of their imaginary outing. It was almost Pavlovian the way a cold shiver would run down all of our spines when one of us yelled for Mom.

My mother sat across the coffee table on a gold velvet couch that was hermetically sealed in plastic. (To keep it fresh, I guess.) It was scorching outside, but in spite of the heat, my mother was poised and regal. She'd been a print model when she was younger, and she always maintained her perfect posture. Her smooth hands, tipped with perfectly manicured nails, rested in her lap, as Tracie and I eagerly awaited her decision on our dispute.

Suddenly, another hand darted into the picture. A bigger hand. Bigger than mine and Tracie's put together. A hand that's known work. Hard work. Grandma's hand.

"Oh, give me the doggone cards!"

Grandma, wearing a flowered dress with a white apron, sat next to my mother on the couch. She'd spent the morning cooking at one of the convalescent hospitals in Oakland and would spend the evening taking care of us. She was capable, no-nonsense.

"I said give *me* the doggone cards!"

Grandma took the cards and dealt them. As always, Tracie had to start trouble.

"Mommy, I don't got no wild cards."

"No, Tracie, it's 'I don't have *any* wild cards.' 'I don't got no' is a double negative, which cancels itself out, so that would mean you *do* have wild cards."

Tracie studied her cards in confusion and then showed them to Mom: "Where?"

"Gal, hold your cards where she can't see 'em," Grandma said, shoving Tracie's cards away from my mother's gaze.

When my family plays five hundred, we play with wild cards. Deuces and jokers are wild; they're worth fifty points and can be used in place of any other card. I was intently studying my cards when I heard a loud *smack*, as though someone has just been slapped in the face. I looked up to see my mother with a joker stuck to her forehead. Whenever she'd get a wild card, she'd stick it to her forehead to psych the rest of us out.

Incidentally, that's one of the joys of being black: oilier skin. It's bad when you're young because of acne, but as you get older, you don't wrinkle. You've heard the expression "Black don't crack"? That's where it comes from.

My wife is my age and Caucasian. She says that forty years from now, she'll look her age, but I'll still look good. When we go places, it'll be like I'm driving Miss Daisy.

Smack! My mother had a joker stuck to her forehead, and all that regal stuff just went right out the window.

"Gal, you got another wild card?" Grandma said. "Shit!"

"Suer!"

My mother never called my grandmother anything other than Suer. Grandma's siblings call her "sister." When my mother was little, it came out as "Suer." It stuck.

"Ooh, Grandma said a bad word!" Tracie intoned, the gleeful profanity police.

"Suer, stop cussing, and Tracie, I told you to call her 'Nana.'"

Tracie, always the shit disturber.

"Mommy, where were you born?"

"Providence, Rhode Island."

My mother always said that, because Providence, Rhode

Island, is where white people come from. There's a factory there where they crank them out on an assembly line.

You see, my mother really wanted white children. I know, I'm stereotyping and profiling here but, come on. She wanted us to call Grandma Nana. Black people don't talk like that.

"Nana, might I trouble you for some more grits, please?"

Never in a million years.

"Providence, Rhode Island," she continued.

Grandma huffed a disgusted, "Shit."

"Suer, I asked you to stop cussing."

"Then quit lying to the gal!"

"Providence, Rhode Island."

"Your ass was born in Birmingham, same as me."

"Providence, Rhode Island," she insisted, gritting her teeth.

"Now you know I ain't never been to no doggone Rhode Island so how in the hell was you born there?"

Now poor Tracie looked back and forth, not knowing what to do. She knew that one of them was lying, and that whichever one she accused, rightly or wrongly, was going to smack her in the mouth. In a white household you call an adult a liar, you get a time out. In a black household, you call an adult a liar, you're lucky if you ever come to. You DO NOT call an adult a liar in a black household.

I decided that I was going to play the peacemaker.

"Well, you know Grandma, maybe you just thought you were in Birmingham but you were really in Providence, Rhode Island. Because in Rhode Island, they put fire hoses and dogs on black people, too, and . . ."

"Boy, hush. That gal was born in Birmingham!"

My mother refused to give in.

"Providence, Rhode Island!"

Our little geographical discussion was interrupted by a

smell that wafted through the room. The musky smell of Brut. You know, that cheap men's cologne. That smell could mean only one thing. Sylvester, my father, would come walking in the house. In about five minutes.

Two years prior, Sylvester had left the house, saying that he was going to the store, and vanished. Three days ago he came walking in the door carrying a bag of groceries and bitching about the long line.

He was always doing things like that. When I was a kid, Sylvester was in the army during the Vietnam War. I swear to you the first military term I ever learned was AWOL. Absent Without Leave. I remember the MPs knocking on the front door.

"We thought he was with you," my mother told them.

Now, Sylvester breezed into the room with his usual greeting.

"What's happening?"

"Mommy was born in Providence, Rhode Island!" Tracie said.

"Shit," Sylvester replied as he walked down the hallway to his bedroom.

During this entire card game, I had been drinking Dad's Old Fashioned Root Beer. It was the only "dad" who had consistently been in my life up to that point.

Is that "black"?

I'd had just about as much root beer as my little eight-year-old bladder could handle so I got up to go to the bathroom. In order to go to the bathroom, I had to walk down the hallway and pass Sylvester's room. As I approached, I was quiet. I was always quiet around him because I was afraid that he'd tell me that I was "cutting my eyes" at him or something. That was a consistent refrain from Sylvester.

"Quit cutting your eyes at me!"

I didn't know what it meant then. I don't know what it means now.

"Quit cutting your eyes at me before I rip 'em out of their goddamned sockets."

I got so I'd just close my eyes around him altogether.

"I'm just here with my dog and my cane, Dad."

"Tell that damn dog to quit cutting his eyes at me!"

Sylvester was crazy. I never knew what he was going to say or what he was going to do. He used to mess with my head.

"Hey, Brian, come here," he'd say.

"Yes, Daddy?"

"Knock, knock."

"Who's there?"

He'd then slap me in the head and say, "What the fuck did I tell you about answering the door when you don't know who's on the other goddamned side of it?"

Once when I was five, I sniffed in a way that Sylvester thought was directed at him. He grabbed my nose and pinched it so hard that it was bruised for a month. When people asked what happened he said, "The boy fell off his tricycle. I told his ass to be careful."

As I approached Sylvester's room, I was quiet. I felt my stomach climb into my throat as I noticed that his damned door was open.

"Hey," he shouted.

"Yes?"

"Quit sticking your lip out at me!"

I've got to tell you that it had been a hard day. The reason for the card game was that I'd come home from school upset and everyone was trying to cheer me up, to distract me. That day at recess I had been playing kickball, and I was the worst. I had no athletic ability whatsoever.

Not black. I told you.

That day, I was in the outfield and this little redheaded kid came up to kick. He was the best kicker in the second grade. You know the one. He got a home run every time he was up. He kicked the ball directly to me and for the first time in my life, I caught it. I actually caught it! Usually it would fall through my arms or bounce off of my chest, but this time I caught it. I was ecstatic. I was elated. I was so happy for about fifteen seconds, until the kid looked me dead in the face and yelled, "Nigger!"

Now, I'd heard the word before, usually from Sylvester. He apparently thought that it was my first name. He was always yelling it at me.

"Nigger, turn that shit down."

"Nigger, close the door, it's cold in here!"

But I'd never heard it like this before. This was different. This hurt.

"Nigger, I said quit sticking you lip out at me," Sylvester screamed.

"Huh?"

"You heard me, motherfucker!"

"I'm not sticking my lip out at you, Daddy. It's the way my lips are made."

I turned and headed down the hallway. I got two, maybe three steps before I heard:

"Motherfucker! You must be crazy talking to me like that. You a man now, motherfucker? Huh? You a man now?"

I was suddenly lying on the floor of the hallway with a grown man on top of me, my father strangling me.

"You a man now? Come on, motherfucker. Talk some more shit. You such a goddamned man, talk some more shit."

Out of nowhere came the voices of my mom, my grandma, and my sister.

"Leave that boy alone!"

"Stop it, you're killing him! You're killing him!"

"Let him go."

I was coughing and crying. I threw up a little bit. Then suddenly it was quiet. Everybody was gone. My head rested in my mother's lap. I guess I must have blacked out.

"It's okay. He's gone," she soothed. "He's gone. I won't let him hurt you. We're going to get away from him. I don't know where but I'll find us a place. Some place. I promise. I promise."

The next day, my mother came walking in the door from work with a big grin on her face. It was as though she had a great big joker stuck to her forehead.

"Guess what?" she said. "We're moving. I found us a place, a nice place. We're going to move to San Leandro."

CHAPTER 2

The Friendly City

The year is 1969. The setting is Dick Linton's auto-body shop. Three white men, Linton, Frank Reis, and David Pedroza, discuss race relations and the state of affairs in their small town.

PEDROZA: Look at those riots. What the [expletive] do you think would happen to us if we went over there and started a riot?

REIS (grinning): They'd kill us.

PEDROZA: [expletive] right they would.

REIS: Paint your face black and you can get a new Cadillac and the county will come in and feed your family. What do they call it? Prejudice or something? That's all they've got to holler and they've got it made. Let a [expletive] policeman stop me and I've got to pay.

PEDROZA (angry): There's only one way to solve this, and that's gonna be with a revolution. I'm for fighting it out between us.

REIS: And I'd go for that. Just give me a machine gun.

LINTON: That's why I went out and bought me some guns.

REIS: We should have a Hitler here to get rid of the troublemakers the way they did with the Jews in Germany.

I know what you're probably thinking. The above exchange took place in Birmingham, right? Or Providence, Rhode Island. Sometimes, even I get confused. But the above exchange actually took place in San Leandro, California, in 1969. *Newsweek* magazine came to town as part of a cover story on Richard Nixon's "forgotten white majority." Which is ridiculous on its face: How do you forget the majority? They're everywhere. That's why they're called "the majority." *Newsweek* talked to these charming gentlemen for its October 6, 1969 edition. The above exchange is quoted verbatim.

San Leandro borders Oakland, to the south. According to the demographic breakdown in the 1970 census, Oakland was nearly half black. San Leandro was 99.99 percent white. That demo hadn't changed since the 1960 census. Ninety-nine point ninety-nine percent.

Ivory Soap looked at that number and went, "WOW!!"

At the Oakland–San Leandro border, at the corner of Durant Street and East 14th Street, there used to be an archway that read, WELCOME TO SAN LEANDRO: THE FRIENDLY CITY. (Interestingly, East 14th is now called International Boulevard, because the city of Oakland was concerned about the fact that East 14th Street was well known for its drug dealers. The city decided something had to be done, so the city council voted to change the name to "International Boulevard." Voila, no more drug dealers on East 14th Street. And the phrase "Just say 'no'" ended all substance abuse among teens. I'll take simple solutions to complex problems for a hundred, Alex.) The "Friendly City" archway was unofficially known by the black residents of East Oakland as "the invisible wall."

A San Leandro patrolman used to sit inside that archway. It was his job to follow any black pedestrian, motorist, or cyclist who crossed over into the city limits. Black drivers had police cars in their rearview mirrors from the moment that they entered town until the moment they left. If they committed the slightest vehicle-code infraction, real or imaginary, they were stopped and directed back across the border to Oakland, "where they belonged." Black children naive enough to breach the wall would find themselves paced by San Leandro P.D. until they retreated.

This was San Leandro, California, located in the "liberal" Bay Area, just twenty miles from San Francisco. Fifteen miles from the U.C. Berkeley campus. Six years after the Summer of Love.

In the mid 1960s, a black doctor who moved to town was greeted with a shotgun blast through his front door. A few years later, the mother of seventeen-year-old Alicia Fields, a white teenager who circulated a petition among the student body of her high school in favor of integrating the campus, wrote a letter to the local paper publicly disowning the girl for daring to suggest such an appalling idea. In 1971, the National Committee Against Discrimination in Housing called San Leandro "a racist bastion of White Supremacy." On Thanksgiving Day of that year, CBS/Westinghouse aired *The Suburban Wall*, a one-hour documentary that highlighted San Leandro's racist practices and blatant, organized campaign to skirt federal fair-housing laws. The U.S. Commission on Civil Rights actually conducted hearings to determine why there existed such a racial disparity between San Leandro and its neighbor to the north.

And then, we moved to town.

We moved to San Leandro on August 2, 1972. It was the city's centennial celebration, commemorating one hundred years since the town was incorporated. It had been a long journey. Like much of what we now know as the United States, San Leandro had started as Indian territory. In the late 1700s, the Spanish arrived and decided that the "savage" native inhabitants needed a conversion to Christianity. The indigenous residents were moved to one of two missions (Mission San Jose and San Francisco's Mission Delores) where their inability to fight off European diseases killed the vast majority of them.

Once the natives were marginalized, various land grants divided the territory into ranches, or ranchos, which were deeded to the Spanish settlers. The ranchos were subsequently bought or squatted on by white settlers from the East looking to make their fortunes supplying goods and services to the people of the burgeoning city of San Francisco. Eventually, this predominantly white population took over, founding businesses and planting orchards. The territory was incorporated as the city of San Leandro on March 21, 1872. Later, Portuguese immigrants—who were willing to work hard and be gouged by grossly inflated prices for land—came to dominate the city. Their descendants populate San Leandro to this day.

San Leandro boasts two claims to fame in the world of entertainment. The first is Hal Peary, who originated the role of Throckmorton P. Gildersleeve on radio in the *Fibber McGee and Molly* show and later on his own program, *The Great Gildersleeve*. Peary was born a third generation San Leandran and raised in the city. The second entertainer was Lloyd Bridges, a versatile film and TV actor best known for the television show *Sea Hunt*. I suppose that an argument could be made that with my choice of profession, I'm carrying on a great tradition. Look at me and my delusions of grandeur.

The city was also ground zero for a major civil rights challenge during World War II. In 1942, San Leandro police arrested a young Japanese-American man named Fred Korematsu for failing to report for internment. After being convicted for knowingly violating the Civilian Exclusion Order, Korematsu appealed his conviction all the way to the United States Supreme Court. The high court upheld the conviction, thus ending all potential challenges to Japanese internment across America. Four decades later, during more tolerant times, Korematsu finally succeeded in having his conviction overturned, receiving an official apology from the U.S. government and a Presidential Medal of Freedom from President Clinton for his persistence in fighting prejudice.

To this day, I don't know how much my mother knew about San Leandro and its reputation when she moved us there. From what I've been able to ascertain, San Leandro's hostility toward blacks was well known among the African-American populations of the neighboring communities of Hayward and Oakland. They spoke of the border as though it were enemy territory.

As one resident of 1970s East Oakland told me, "You just knew not to go there."

Then again, my mother didn't really associate with the black community. She truly could have been oblivious to the hostility blacks faced in the city; on the other hand, San Leandro may have been as close to her vision of Providence, Rhode Island, as she could find in the East Bay. "I'm not one of *those* blacks."

The place my mother had found was located in Washington Manor, a tract of homes in the southwestern part of town that was developed to accommodate the large number of young families migrating to the suburbs following World War II. Most of the breadwinners brought home their bacon by working in manufacturing jobs at one of the many plants in the city, including Caterpillar Tractor (founded in San Leandro) and Golden Grain. For a long time, Rice-A-Roni, "the San Francisco treat," was actually made in San Leandro. (I suppose "the San Leandro treat" doesn't have quite the same cachet.)

By the 1960s, many of San Leandro's residents had moved

there from Oakland, where they'd grown up prior to the war. Before World War II, Oakland had been primarily white, but once the conflict ended, scores of Southern blacks who had been stationed in the Bay Area decided to stay. This, of course, meant that they had to have some place to live. This provided a golden opportunity for enterprising Realtors: blockbusting. It's almost hard to believe this practice existed as I write this at the dawn of the twenty-first century, but at that time, blockbusting was a common practice in many parts of America. The way it worked was brilliant in its simplicity.

A Realtor would go into a white neighborhood and offer a homeowner an inflated price for his house. The homeowner, feeling as though he'd just won the lottery, would jump at the quick profit. The Realtor would then sell the house (often at a loss) to the first black home-buyer he could find. The remaining white homeowners in the neighborhood would be aghast at the prospect of "undesirables" moving in and "lowering the property values," so they would dump their homes to the Realtor at a discount. The Realtor would then resell to black home-buyers. The resulting "white flight" would make the Realtor a fortune, while turning the fear of falling property values into a self-fulfilling prophecy.

Once they sold their homes, the white population needed a place to go. That's where San Leandro came in.

M.C. Friel, a white real estate broker from the neighboring town of Hayward, had made a fortune with his plan to create and maintain lily-white communities. Race covenants, which barred the transfer of property to nonwhites, had been in place in California since the turn of the twentieth century. Back then, there had been a great migration of Chinese immigrants moving into San Francisco, working to build the railroads and other industrial businesses. Many white citizens did not particularly care for the idea of Chinese neighbors, so these covenants were put on the deeds of many of the properties. Although a 1948 U.S. Supreme Court ruling (Shelly v. Kraemer) invalidated such covenants, many California homes continue to have the unenforceable restrictions on their titles.

Friel came up with a way to get around the Supreme Court by forming homeowners' associations in communities throughout the Bay Area. Through legal mumbo jumbo, these associations held the authority to arbitrarily decide who was a suitable homeowner for their respective areas and who wasn't. In 1948, Friel was able to convince the San Leandro Chamber of Commerce to get on board with his plans to ban "the great influx" of Negro families locating in the area since the war.

San Leandro's ten homeowners' associations, representing nearly two-thirds of all property owners, colluded to restrict the presence of blacks in the city. The associations decided who would be on the city council and then pressured council members to reject any proposal that would make it easier for people of color to locate there. Their restrictive practices included agreements by member homeowners not to sell or show their homes to blacks. San Leandro's homeowners' associations would keep a stranglehold on the city council and public policy for more than a generation.

In fairness, San Leandro was not the only California town struggling with the issue of integration during this time. In 1963, W. Byron Rumford, a Berkeley pharmacist and the third African American elected to the State Assembly in California, got the state legislature to pass the Rumford Act, which made it illegal to discriminate in housing on the basis of race, creed, or color. When Governor Edmund "Pat" Brown signed the legislation into law, Realtors across the state went ballistic.

The real estate industry created the Proposition 14 initiative and got it on the 1964 ballot. Prop 14 repealed Rumford. The rationale used to help bigots feel better about being bigots was that this was a "property rights" issue. The government has no business telling you that you can't sell or rent to whomever you wish. Proposition 14 passed by a 2-to-1 margin statewide. The only city to reject it was Berkeley. In 1966, the California State Supreme Court invalidated the initiative when it ruled Prop 14 unconstitutional and in violation of the Civil Rights Act of 1964.

While you may be able to legislate behavior, you can't legislate sentiments or attitudes. As Martin Luther King Jr. once said during the Civil Rights Movement, "The law can't make a man love me but it can sure stop him from lynching me."

When Ronald Reagan ran for California governor in 1966, one of the centerpieces of his campaign was a pledge to overturn Rumford. In other words, "Vote for me and I'll make it legal for you to discriminate." He won, but was unable to circumvent federal law to keep that pledge. That didn't, however, stop communities like San Leandro from using other methods to maintain their all-white status.

Well, almost all-white, that is. Until August 2, 1972, when the Copelands moved to town.

CHAPTER 3

In the Beginning

"They (blacks) are qualified to live in San Leandro if they're willing to accept the kind of life that we have here, which is just an average, ordinary, middle-class American community."

—Frank King, executive vice president,
San Leandro Chamber of Commerce, 1971

The place my mother had moved us to was a hundred-unit apartment complex at the corner of Washington and Fargo Avenues. The complex was called Kendon Village and was comprised of about a dozen antiseptically clean, lime-green buildings.

My first Saturday in San Leandro, I was awakened by a beam of sunlight on my face, so warm it felt like it was being focused through a magnifying glass. The smell of freshly cut grass perfumed the air. We'd been in San Leandro almost a week and all I'd done was mope. I wasn't happy to be "the new kid" again. We had moved a lot, five times in the previous three years. I was born in Akron, Ohio, and lived there until I was five. Midway into my kindergarten year, we packed up and moved to Killeen, Texas to be near Ft. Hood and Sylvester. During one of Mom and Sylvester's splits, we moved to Berkeley. From there to the rough part of East Oakland, eventually escaping to Hayward. Now, San Leandro. I'd spent my life as "the new kid." I hated it.

My mother poked her head in the bedroom door.

"Oh good, honey, you're up. Listen, we're almost unpacked. Why don't you go out and explore? Meet some of the kids around here and introduce yourself. I hear there's a park nearby."

I climbed out of bed, put on my clothes, brushed my teeth, grabbed my bat and baseball, and headed for the door.

"It'll be okay, honey," she said. "Remember, you're the man of the house now."

Maybe it would be okay. Sylvester wasn't there. How bad could it be?

I ambled down the street, taking in the Donna Reed/*Father Knows Best*/*My Three Sons* ambiance. It was clean. Small houses, neat lawns. The elementary school was right next door. That was good. Yeah. This was okay. I started to relax.

My sense of comfort disappeared with a squeal of tires as a shiny blue convertible jolted to a stop beside me. It was a neat old car, a gleaming amalgamation of sky-blue steel and chrome. The wheels sported old-fashioned tires with the wide white walls exaggerated around their circumference. The obligatory fuzzy dice swung to and fro as they dangled from the rearview mirror. Six teenagers were piled into the vehicle. Three boys, three girls. They looked like they had just left a pep rally at Archie's Riverdale High. The boys had on letterman's jackets that read REBELS. I didn't think this was a good sign, but I was eight and I was friendly.

"Hi," I said in my best Beaver Cleaver voice.

A boy in the passenger seat spoke up, his face so covered with acne it looked like a relief map.

"Oakland's that way," he chuckled, pointing to the north.

His friends laughed.

I tried to be nice again.

"Can you please tell me how to get to the park?"

"What for? They don't allow no niggers in that park!"

His friends laughed again.

" 'They don't allow no' is a double negative, which cancels itself out so that means they *do* allow niggers in that park."

I thought that was damned quick for an eight-year-old if I do say so myself. His friends laughed. He'd just been topped by a kid. A black kid.

I watched as his face changed from that of a tormentor with an innate sense of superiority to that of a humiliated fool.

"They don't allow no niggers on this street, either!"

Okay, I didn't really have a comeback for that one. Or what came next.

"Let's kick his ass!"

I didn't really hear all of that last sentence. I'd taken off running somewhere between the words "kick" and "his."

I darted across the street as I heard the engine gun and the tires squeal. I cut across one of the neatly manicured lawns and took a quick right turn, and then, up ahead, I saw it. A police car. Thank God, I was saved.

As I approached, a tall blond cop got out. He was wearing a pair of those mirrored sunglasses that were oh so "cop chic" in the seventies. As I ran toward him, he put his hand on his gun.

"All right, where do you think you're going?"

My heart was pounding a mile a minute. I could barely breathe.

"Those . . . kids . . . are . . . chasing . . . me. They're . . . going . . . to . . . beat . . . me . . . up!"

He paused for a minute and I thought that he was going to

ask me for a description or which way they went, or . . . well, you know where this is going, don't you?

Black readers: "Uh-huh."

White readers: "What? You mean that the policeman isn't going to help the little Negro boy??"

I'm kidding. I know that you're hip to this stuff, which is why you forked over your hard-earned cash to buy this diatribe. I also know that you've heard stories like this a thousand times. A hundred thousand times. The problem is that, no matter how many times you hear these stories, you can't understand them if you haven't lived through them. You just can't. I like to equate it to Vietnam.

You'll hear these guys go, "Yep. I know all about Vietnam."

"Oh, really? Where'd you serve?"

"Well . . . I saw a documentary on the History Channel."

My absolute favorites are those white guys who'll try to empathize with you.

"Yeah, man. I know exactly what you go through, man. I've got long hair and the cops hassle me, too."

"Well cut your fucking hair so the cops quit hassling you!"

Come on, now.

These stories all have the same basic elements if you are a black male in this society, be you eight, eighteen, twenty-eight, thirty-eight, walking, riding your bike, driving your car, or running from angry kids who want to kill you. The first question is always the same.

"Do you have any identification?"

I'm eight!!

"All right, where'd you get the bat and ball?"

"I got it at Sears. I used my birthday money. My sister wanted to come but . . ."

"Do you have a receipt?"

What are you? My accountant?

"All right, where do you live?"

"In Kendon Village."

After an eerie silence, he muttered, "*Which* Kendon Village?"

You mean, there's more than one?

"The green apartments around here . . . someplace."

"You know, maybe you'd better show me."

He gestured toward the police car and I reached for the passenger side door. Just as I was about to touch the handle, he stopped me.

"Just a minute," he barked.

He took my bat and ball, put them on the hood of the squad car, and then I was officially baptized as a black male in this society. He had me raise my hands over my head and he patted me down. I was eight years old.

I could feel my stomach churn. I staved off fear with sarcastic thoughts that I was smart enough not to articulate verbally.

"Gee," I thought, "I sure hope he doesn't find the grenades I'm carrying. What does he think I am? A midget Black Panther, an outside agitator here to start a militant school-lunch program in his town or something?"

Once he was satisfied that I wasn't armed, he again gestured to the police car. I again reached for the passenger side door. Again, he stopped me. This was getting monotonous.

"Uh-uh. Back here," he said, putting me in the backseat.

If you've ever been in the back of a police car, the first thing you notice is that there are no door handles. There are no mechanisms for rolling the window up and down. It can't be opened from the inside. A plexiglass shield separates the backseat from the front. I looked around, wondering if all of the spirits of all of the bad people who had sat in this confined space were channeling through me. Was I a bad person now?

When I was a kid, I used to catch butterflies and put them in Grandma's mayonnaise jars. People would say, "Let it go. That's cruel!"

"Well, I poked holes in the top. He can breathe."

Now, I was the butterfly. And just being able to breathe was not enough.

He pulled into the parking lot of the apartment complex and I directed him to my building. He parked, let me out of the backseat, grabbed my bat, and headed for the door. He knocked. My mother answered.

"Brian . . . Officer? Is there a problem?"

I was too petrified to speak. I wanted to say something but the words just wouldn't come out of my larynx. The cop's vocal cords worked fine.

"Are you this young man's mother?"

"Yes."

"And you live . . . here?"

She was exasperated, I could tell. Did she know what was going on here?

"Yes. What's the problem?"

He paused for a moment as if contemplating his next words.

"He was running around the neighborhood causing trouble."

I could feel my larynx heal. The power of a false accusation can sometimes work wonders.

"I wasn't! Mom, I wasn't!"

He thrust my bat toward her.

"He was using this as a weapon. That's very serious."

"Mom . . . I wasn't! I wasn't!"

This was weird. I knew that kids would lie on other kids to get them in trouble. I mean, I've got sisters, after all. I didn't know that grown-ups did it, too. I didn't know that policemen did it.

Then, I realized something. I was all of four-foot-nothing. He was a six-foot-two cop. He had a police car. He had a baton. He had handcuffs. He had a radio that he could use to call for more policemen with more police cars and more batons. He had a gun. He had bullets. And . . . he was afraid of me.

I could barely make out his words as his eyes blazed with a strange blend of fury and panic. I could see the beads of sweat on his upper lip dancing in time to the music from some bizarre ballet as he admonished my mother.

"This is a very quiet neighborhood and we aim to keep it that way. I'd suggest in the future that you keep a close eye on your son."

My mother gently put her hand on my shoulder and nudged me in the door. She was actually polite to the bastard.

"Thank you for bringing him home."

She was a class act to the bitter end.

Without saying a word, I ran upstairs to my room and buried my face in my pillow. Those kids. Sylvester. That cop. What was it about my very existence that so offended people?

The question did not bring tears. Instead, it brought darkness. It was dark all around me. It was a beautiful August day with a blazing afternoon sun, yet all around me was an inky molasses that I'd never encountered before. I didn't know what it was. I didn't know how long it would last. All I knew was that it made me not want to do *anything*, ever again.

My mother called from downstairs.

"Honey, I'm going to the store. Do you want to come with me? I'll buy you some comic books?"

"No, thank you. I'm just gonna stay in my room."

"Hey, Brian, come on down here and play cards with me."

"No, Grandma. I just want to stay in here."

"Honey, we're going to go get hamburgers. I'll buy you some root beer . . ."

"You guys go on ahead. I'm not hungry. I just want to be by myself."

CHAPTER 4

Thirty-five Candles

Q: What do you call a black multimillionaire Industrialist?
A: A nigger.

—Old Joke

It was a quarter to midnight as I sat in the sports bar with my buddies drinking shots of Irish whiskey. Jameson. I love Jameson. It's so smooth, it goes down like water. Well, it goes down like water until the burn hits your chest and then it feels like you've just ingested hydrochloric acid. I felt like I could handle a few more burns though. It was early yet and it was a special occasion. My wife had given me a kitchen pass. She'd watch our children while I celebrated.

Fifteen minutes to go until my birthday. Thirty-five. I would be thirty-five and still here in good old San Leandro. I'd hit my mid-thirties. How the hell had I reached my mid-thirties? I was just trying to buy beer with a fake ID the day before yesterday.

The ID worked, too. Well, I should say that it worked in most places. I picked it up from a place on University Avenue in Berkeley that had, shall we say, "relaxed" standards for the documentation they required to process your identification card. Mine read that I was Dr. Copeland from Canton, Ohio. It worked like a charm and was only questioned once.

Senior year in high school, I flashed it to a security guard at Harvey's Casino in Lake Tahoe. He'd been watching me nervously put quarters into a slot machine for a half hour. It was my first time in a casino and I was terrified of getting caught gambling. My hands were shaking so much that I was actually dropping the quarters on the floor as I aimed for the coin slot. The guard watched me like a hawk, smiling. He even waved at me once.

"This is cool," I thought.

Right up until the moment that I hit a hundred-dollar jackpot. Then the story changed.

"May I see some identification?" The guard asked, having bolted to my side, making sure to catch me before I started putting coins in my pocket.

It was a good feeling to be asked that question by a white man in a uniform and actually be able to comply for once, as precarious as the compliance may have been.

I flashed him my fake ID card. He took it and held it up to the light, studying it. I don't think they scrutinize IDs like this today in post–9/11, high-security situations. At the airport, they'll make me take off my shoes and wand my laptop, but my ID could have bin Laden's picture and still get through most checkpoints.

Finally the guard smirked and said, "Dr. Copeland, huh?"

"That's right."

"You look a little young to be a doctor."

"Child prodigy," I blurted out. It sounded logical. To me anyhow. Seventeen-year-old "logic."

The friendly, waving guard was gone. He had morphed into a hard-ass guard.

"We see these up here all the time," he grunted.

"Look, that is a legal identification card," I protested.

Good, Brian. Argue with him, you knucklehead. You're a black kid in ski country. Black teenagers who ski, now there's a short list.

Hey, I just realized: I don't ski. That's black!

The guard stroked his chin.

"I'll tell you what."

"What?" I said anxiously. I wanted my hundred bucks.

"You have two choices. I can call the police and have them come down here to verify this card, and when they determine that it's a fake, you can go to jail . . ."

"Or?" I asked, choice one not sounding too appealing.

"You can walk out of here right now without the card and without the money."

Without missing a beat I said, "You have a nice day, sir," as I calmly strolled out the door.

I can make good decisions when I want to.

Now, I'm in my mid-thirties. Nobody cards me anymore. Twenty-year-olds accidentally bump into me and say, "Excuse me, sir."

Sir. When did I become a "Sir"? Who the fuck am I, Sidney Poitier?

My friends in my age range all began to lament the drag of not being twenty-one anymore. It was one of those drunken conversations that guys have when boozy saturation gives way to melancholic reflection. These conversations get deep and philosophical. They progress to hugs and "I love you man's" until somebody has to run to the bathroom and puke. Sometimes it's me. The one good thing about hair like mine is that your friends don't have to hold it back for you when you're heaving your guts out into the toilet. There are pluses.

My buddy Mark always gets the most sentimental at these times.

Mark is a year older than me and has been my big brother since he took me under his wing when we were in high school. Back then, Mark was the good-looking white guy who got all of the hot girls. I was "Mark's friend." This meant that I was responsible for awkwardly keeping his dates' friends occupied while he "occupied" his date. That was my role on double dates. Julie your Cruise Director. It had been Mark who took me to Berkeley for my liquor-store M.D.

"When," Mark asked, "did you first realize that you were an adult?"

The guys go around the table.

"When I graduated high school," one said.

"When I got married," came another reply.

"When I first got my own place."

"When I filed my first tax return."

"When my first kid was born."

After everybody had spoken, they all looked at me.

"How about you, Brian? When did you first realize that you were all grown up?"

I didn't want to go there. I can't go there. I won't.

"Speaking of childhood, I have to go to the bathroom before I do a very childish thing," I said, forever the joker.

The guys all laughed as I excused myself from the table and headed into the restroom.

I walked into the men's room and went into one of the stalls. I hate public bathrooms. I'm like Howard Hughes about that kind of stuff. I don't touch the door to the bathroom because guys pee without washing their hands and then use the door knob. I won't touch the handle to the stall with my bare hands. When I have to sit (which I try to avoid at all costs) I quadruple paper the seat and the floor in front of me. I think I finally understand that "hover" thing that my sister says women have to do in situations like this. It keeps them germ-free and builds strong quads.

After going through my usual motions to make the conditions around me as sanitary as possible under the circumstances, I heard the door open, followed by the voices of two guys, apparently just as boozy as my little entourage. I couldn't see them, but I could hear every word.

"Your team sucks, man."

"Only because our regular pitcher is out. Otherwise we'd have kicked your asses all over the field. Don't get cocky."

"You're still buying the beers. I don't give a rat's ass what your excuse is. You lost and I want Coronas."

"You'll get your fucking Coronas."

"With lime, asshole."

"Yeah, yeah. With lime. Beer with lime in it. You pussy."

"I am what I eat."

Charming fellows. They prattled on.

"Hey, did you see who's here?"

"Who?"

"Brian Copeland."

"Really? Where?"

"He's sitting at a table in the corner with a bunch of guys. You went to school with him, didn't you?"

"Yeah."

"He seems to be doing okay for himself. I see him on TV. Me and Carrie saw him open for Earth Wind & Fire in Vegas at Caesar's."

"Yeah."

"It looks like he's doing really well."

"So?"

"So? That's all you got to say is 'so'?"

"What else is there to say? He's still a nigger."

I heard the guys laugh. They finished their business and went out the door. I didn't hear water running. More justification for not touching the doorknob on the way out.

Their words reverberated in my head.

"He's still a nigger."

I'd worked my ass off, built a life and a family, I was thirty-five years old and I was "still a nigger."

I pasted on my fake, TV smile and rejoined my party. Someone yelled that it was one minute after midnight. The guys lined up three and a half shots of Jameson for me, one for each decade of my life, with half a shot for the last five years. I downed them as the guys sang "Happy Birthday." What's so damned happy about it?

As I finished, the waitress brought me another whiskey.

"This is from the gentleman at the bar," she said, gesturing.

I looked over to see two guys sitting on bar stools, including a guy I knew from grade school. A guy I hadn't seen in years. A guy who's voice was still in my head.

"He's still a nigger."

He raised his glass in my direction in a toast.

"Happy Birthday," he shouted from across the room.

I didn't say a word. I simply raised my drink in his direction returning the toast. Then, I drained the glass. I'm gonna hate myself in the morning. I can tell, because I hate myself now.

CHAPTER 5

Just a Trim

I didn't venture far from home after the police episode. It wasn't safe. I spent most of the rest of August in the apartment either reading my comics alone in my room, playing games with my sisters, or watching television. My self-imposed exile came to an end one Saturday, when Grandma announced that since school was starting soon, I'd need to get a haircut. Every new school year started with a haircut and a new pair of shoes. It was tradition. Grandma believed that these two things were the keys to success.

"As long as your head and your feet look all right, you okay," she'd say.

I had a regular barber in Oakland. Mr. Johnson at Johnson's Barbershop had been cutting my hair since I was a first grader. His son Joseph and I had been in class together. So when it came time for me to get a trim, we patronized his place.

I grabbed a couple of comic books to read while I waited for my turn in the chair and announced, "Okay, I'm ready to go see Mr. Johnson."

"I don't want you to go to Mr. Johnson's anymore," Mom said.

"Why?"

"We live in a new community and we need to support the

merchants here," she said. "Suer, find someplace to get his hair cut in San Leandro."

"Shit," Grandma said as she opened the front door and headed to the car with me in tow.

Grandma started the engine, backed our new Chevrolet Malibu out of its parking stall, and headed toward the street. She stopped at the driveway entrance and began to turn right. Suddenly she slammed on the brakes. A late model sedan sped up the street right in front of us. As it passed, the pretty young white woman behind the wheel rolled down her window and screamed, "Go back to Oakland!"

"You go to shit!" Grandma yelled back.

I wanted to go back inside. I started to think that this was a bad idea.

"Where are we going, Grandma?"

"I don't know."

"Do you know where the barbershops are around here?"

"Boy, I said, 'I don't know'!" she snapped.

I knew to shut up when she got like this. I was quiet as she headed toward the downtown area. Soon we saw a shopping center. Grandma parked and we got out. She grabbed me by the wrist with a viselike grip. Grandma never held my hand, she held my wrist. She said, "That way you can't run no place."

We walked around the center until we saw the red and white swirl of a barber pole. We walked into an environment so sterile it looked like a NASA decontamination chamber. Everything looked spit-shined. The chrome was sparkling and the mirrors and glass didn't have a smudge or a fingerprint on them. Even though the barber chairs were full and the barbers were furiously working away, there wasn't any hair on the floor. I'd never seen anything like it.

There was a boisterous chatter as Grandma and I walked in.

There was laughing, talking, and storytelling amid the buzz of the electric clipper and the *snip snip snip*ping of scissors. It was a symphony orchestra of various voices and sounds. A symphony that stopped the second we set foot inside the door. It was like those old commercials where E.F. Hutton just spoke and everybody wanted to hear what it was that he was going to say. The entire sea of white faces seemed to be waiting for some words of wisdom from us.

A gray-haired barber in a blue smock abruptly stopped cutting the hair of the little boy perched in a red removable riser on the barber chair. He shut off the clippers and held them suspended in midair as he looked us over. Then . . . he smiled.

"May I help you?" he said, the word "help" taking on a friendliness in the tone he used.

Grandma didn't smile. She looked back at him, hard, stern.

"He need to get his hair cut," she said in her no-nonsense way.

"I'm sorry," the barber said, still smiling. "We don't cut his kind of hair."

He pointed to a sign on the wall that read, NO NATURALS, NO RELAXERS. Why didn't the signs just say, NO BLACKS OR ART GARFUNKELS ALLOWED?

"We don't know how to cut that type of hair," he said, still smiling.

I could feel the stares of the other patrons boring into me, each set of eyes a pair of hot, miniature drills cutting me, searing me.

"Can't help you," he continued. "Sorry."

Grandma's grip on my wrist tightened as she turned on her heels and headed back out the door.

"You might try one of the shops in Oakland," I heard him call out as the din of the symphony resumed.

Grandma was quiet as she stomped back to the Malibu.

"Shit," I heard her mutter under her breath.

We spent the next hour driving around town, stopping at every barber pole we saw. Some barbers smiled like the first guy. Some were icy. The tone and the words were different but at the same time identical in meaning.

"Can't help you."

"I can't handle his hair."

"We don't know how to cut that."

"I'd try one of the places over in Oakland."

"Shit," Grandma said over and over again.

She pointed the car north, drove up to MacArthur Boulevard, and headed toward the city limits.

"Go back to Oakland!" that white woman had shouted from her car window. "Go back to where you belong."

At the Oakland/San Leandro border, there was a noticeable difference in the way that the streets were kept. Upon crossing the line into Oakland, the sidewalk turned from disinfected, antiseptic cleanliness to urban disarray. Where there had been spotless, steam-cleaned streets, there was now a morass of broken glass. Discarded paper and trash lined the street, right up to the ENTERING SAN LEANDRO sign. It was as though even the refuse knew that it was okay to clutter the streets of Oakland, as long as it didn't breach the invisible wall.

The cars parked along MacArthur were old. The faces of the pedestrians changed. They went from shades ranging from lily white and pink to various hues of brown. Light brown, dark brown, ebony. Some as black as tar.

We found a place in front of Mr. Johnson's shop, parked, and went in. We heard the loud voices the second we got out of the car. It was a din like that in the barbershops across the border that we'd just visited, but I immediately noticed that there was something different here. It was dissimilar in a way that I couldn't really describe. Their laughter was rich. The voices were louder, more coarse. They argued and talked over one another with forthrightness. There was animated vulgarity.

There was also an odor. The other shops had no smell. Breathing in them was like taking a big whiff from a head of lettuce. In here, there was a fragrance. The aroma of strong cologne, shaving cream, hair relaxing chemicals, Dixie Peach hair pomade, and burned hair. It didn't exactly smell bad, but it was no bouquet of roses either.

A middle-aged black man stood in the center of the shop, flailing his arms about as his voice got higher and louder. He was dressed poorly. Whereas the patrons in the San Leandro shops were neatly groomed, even before their hair was trimmed, this man was disheveled. He had a head of long, nappy hair that looked dirty even from my vantage point. His face sported a ragged, uneven beard. He wore a sweatshirt that was so dirty it looked like it could have crawled onto his lean frame by itself. As he pontificated, I noticed the yellow glint of gold from one of his front teeth. The other front tooth was missing.

"You can't trust any of those motherfuckers," he shouted.

Mr. Johnson looked up from the head he was shearing as Grandma and I walked in.

"Watch your mouth," he said to the man. "We got kids in here."

"It ain't like he ain't heard this shit before. Is it boy?" he said to me.

I didn't know what to say. I had heard the word "motherfucker" before. Sylvester was my father, after all. I looked at the man and shrugged.

"He need to get his hair cut for school," Grandma said, rescuing me.

"All right. I'll get to him in a minute," Mr. Johnson said, his clippers shaving a tiny wedge of gray hair from the head of the elderly gentleman sitting in his barber chair.

As Grandma and I sat down, I opened one of my Superboy comics and began to read.

"What you reading, young man?" the gold-toothed wonder asked.

"*Superboy*."

Of all my comic book heroes, Superboy would grow to become my favorite. We related to each other. Here was a boy who was truly the only one of his kind in the universe. There was no one else remotely like him. No one with whom he could talk with a common frame of reference. He was just like me. I lived in a house with all females. There were no black men in my life, certainly no black men who could understand what it was like to be the *only* black male in a room, a store, or on a street.

In his guise as young Clark Kent, Superboy had to go to Smallville High and pretend he was just like everybody else. Worse, he had to pretend to be less than everybody else, lest they suspect his secret true identity and be afraid of him. He pretended to be weaker than he was. He pretended to be afraid of spiders. He would deliberately miss questions on tests so as not to get perfect scores and stand out. He longed to belong. He longed for normalcy. Just like me.

"Superboy? He's white, ain't he? What you reading about white boys for?"

"Leave him alone," Mr. Johnson said.

"I'm just talking to the young man." He turned to me. "Why don't you read some books about brothers?"

I shrugged again.

"See?" he said, gesticulating wildly again. "They got our

kids so messed up they don't even know why they do half the shit they do."

"Who is 'they'?" I asked, already sorry that I'd opened my mouth.

I know that there are times when you should never ask questions, because you'll regret it. Never ask old people how they are, because they'll *tell* you. Every ailment, every ache and pain, every grievance they have with their son who doesn't call and their daughter who wants to put them in the home. This guy was one of those. He wasn't exactly old, but I knew that now he'd never shut up.

"*Who*," he said, "is the white folks. The crackers. The peckerwoods. Ofays. Whitey. The Man."

"I said to leave the boy alone," Mr. Johnson said again.

"Why can't I talk to the young man? I might be able to teach him something. Young man, what's your name?"

"Brian."

"Okay, Brian. Let me tell you something. There ain't no white man who is worth a shit. They are your enemy. They will keep a nigger down any chance they get."

"I don't think that's true." Why can't I just shut up so he will, too?

"Name me one white man who's worth a goddamn."

I paused for a moment to think. My experiences with white men hadn't exactly been positive as of late.

"How about George Washington? What about all of those people they put on money? They had to be good to be put on money."

Here we go.

"Money?" He laughed. "Money? Let me tell you something young man. When people talk about a fistful of dollars, they really should be talking about a fistful of bigots. That's all they holding in they're hands. A bunch of bigoted, good for nothing motherfuckers."

"I don't want to have to tell you again to watch your mouth in here, Lester," Mr. Johnson said, getting mad.

His name was Lester. He looked like a Lester. It's weird when people fit their names.

"Okay, okay," Lester said. "Just let me educate y'all. School is officially open. Now, young man. Who is on the hundred-dollar bill?"

I had just seen my first hundred. When I went to the bank with Mom to cash her paycheck, they gave her one. She let me hold it. It looked and smelled different from other money. I wanted them. Lots of them.

"Benjamin Franklin," I answered.

"Benjamin Franklin," Lester said. "Inventor of the lightning rod, inventor of the bifocals, inventor of the Franklin stove. Racist bastard. He had slaves."

"No, he did not!" the old man in the barber chair protested.

"Read your history. He had slaves. Two of 'em. Man and a woman. Woman was actually named Jemima. Motherfucker must have liked pancakes. The only reason that kite he flew in the lightning storm had a key on the end of it was because he couldn't find a nigger small enough to tie on there. Racist."

The man in the chair rolled his eyes.

"Who is on the fifty?" Lester asked, turning to me.

I knew this one, too. I'd actually had a fifty once. I took all of my birthday money, added it to my chore money, and had it changed for a fifty. I carried it around in my pocket for four months before I finally broke it. It was fun saying, "All I have is a fifty."

"President Grant," I shouted, like I was winning a game show quiz.

He nodded.

"Ulysses Simpson Grant. President of the United States. General of the Union Army, fighting for the rights of all them poor slaves. That's what they taught you in school, ain't it? Well, what they didn't teach you is that slaves wiped his sorry ass from the day he was born until he went in the army. Once he was in there, his ass was too drunk to know who the fuck he was helping free."

"You are amazing," Mr. Johnson said with disgust.

"The twenty?" he asked me.

"Andrew Jackson," I shouted. I was even amazing myself. I didn't know I knew so much about money.

"Old Hickory," Lester intoned. "He didn't have slaves. That's because he was too busy killing every motherfucking Indian he could find. You kill enough Indians, boy, and maybe they'll put your ass on the twenty."

"Alexander Hamilton is on the ten-dollar bill," I volunteered.

"Secretary of the Treasury. Shot to death by Vice President Aaron Burr. The only vice president to actually do something. Most of 'em just go to funerals. This motherfucker *caused* funerals."

"Now, I happen to know," the man in the barber chair said, "that Alexander Hamilton did not own slaves. In fact, he was opposed to slavery."

"That's right," Lester shouted. "He was against slavery. But did he say anything about it? Nope. Nothing. Not a goddamned word. He wanted to be secretary of the Treasury.

"Hmm," Lester mocked. "Let me think. I can talk about what bullshit slavery is, or I can have a government job. You niggers better go sing some more spirituals."

Mr. Johnson again rolled his eyes. He'd given up.

"What about the five-dollar bill?" I asked.

Lester stopped dead in his tracks. He was actually silent for a moment.

"Let's talk about the two-dollar bill," he said.

"They don't even make two-dollar bills anymore!" the man in the chair shouted.

Lester ignored him.

"Thomas Jefferson. Third president of the United States. Author of the Declaration of Independence. Son of a bitch not only had slaves, he fucked 'em. Repeatedly. Had kids with them. Not that his continental ass would publicly own up to any of them."

"Lester," Mr. Johnson said, trying hard to control his growing fury, "you use that word in here one more time and you are out the door. I mean it."

"Okay, okay," he said. "Thomas Jefferson. We hold these truths to be self-evident that all men are created equal . . . 'cept niggers. Jefferson had black kids. They had to work for his ass for free though. His slaves weren't even set free when he died. They went to pay off his debts. How'd you like that, boy? Having your ass used to pay off some white man's I.O.U."

"George Washington was still a great man," I said. "He was the first president."

"Yep," Lester says. "First president. General of the continental army. Signer of the Declaration of Independence. Tobacco farmer. And who do you think was farming that tobacco while he was doing all that shit? Niggers."

He stood on the chair next to me as if it were a stage.

"George, did you chop down that cherry tree?" he said. "Father, I cannot tell a lie. The niggers did it!"

The man in the chair shook his head.

"Lester, you are just impossible."

"No, I'm honest. White men ain't worth a shit."

He climbed down off of the chair and started for the door.

"I'll see you uneducated motherfuckers later. I'm leaving so I can say it," he said before Mr. Johnson could protest.

He got to the doorway, walked out, and then turned around and came back in.

"Can somebody lend me a dollar?"

An hour later, I walked into the apartment, my hair neatly cut.

"It looks great!" My mother beamed. "Where did you take him, Suer?"

"To Mr. Johnson's shop."

"What? I told you to take him someplace here in San Leandro."

"There ain't no place in San Leandro," she shouted.

"Do you mean to tell me that there isn't a barbershop in the whole city?"

"Not that will work on black boys."

My mother fell silent. She looked at the floor for a moment, then sighed a deep sigh. A cleansing breath for her soul. After what seemed like an eternity, she spoke.

"You look nice, Brian."

CHAPTER 6

The Hobby Shop

've got three kids. Adam, my oldest, was born on my twenty-fifth birthday. I came into fatherhood without a lot of knowledge because I didn't exactly have a good example. In fact, the only advice that I ever got on parenting came from my friend Steve who said,

"Raising kids is just like making pancakes. You always mess up the first one."

Gee, that's comforting. Thank you very much. I appreciate that.

Adam was four years old and we were in the minivan. I was driving. Adam sat in the back strapped in his little car seat. I saw in the rearview mirror that he was cutting his eyes at me. I let it go. I'm the anti-Sylvester. He'd better not stick his lip out.

We were on our way to the hobby shop to get Adam some finger paints. As if he didn't have enough crap at home to make it a mess, I was now actually going out to buy shit to bring home to make the house messy.

We went into this San Leandro hobby shop that I loved. I dig hobby shops and this one was really cool. It was a cavern filled with radio-controlled cars and helicopters, and model airplanes, rockets, sailboats, and railroads. It was a magical place. With a little imagination my son and I could be anything that we wanted to be. We were race-car drivers and astronauts, chopper pilots and engineers. For me, the hobby shop was always a portal for dreams.

Adam was at least as excited as I was as he ran up and down the aisles. He suddenly stopped to study a scale model of a B-1 Bomber.

"Daddy, what are those things coming out of the back of the airplane?"

"They're bombs."

"Bombs? What are they for?"

I pondered the appropriate response for a four-year-old before blurting out, "Making defense contractors rich. Now, come on. Let's go get your finger paints."

I had been reading all of this stuff about how war toys make little boys more aggressive, so I wouldn't even let him have those little green plastic army men that burned so well when I was a kid. Ah, memories.

It's really important to me to be a good dad. I figure that since Sylvester was such a horrible, fucked-up individual, if I can just do the opposite of what he did, I'll be like Cosby and Fred MacMurray all rolled into one. I do things that Sylvester didn't do, like coming home from the store.

He didn't work so I work a lot. He didn't spend time with his kids, so I do.

Adam got his finger paints and we were up at the cash register where I was fishing for my credit card to pay, when I noticed that Adam was mesmerized by a display model of a dollhouse.

"My ONLY son is fascinated by a dollhouse!!"

I thought, "Maybe I need to rethink this war toys position of mine."

I stopped myself. "No, no. I'm a tolerant Bay Area parent. I'm a tolerant Bay Area parent. I'll keep saying it to myself until

I actually believe it. I'm a tolerant Bay Area parent and it's important for him to grow up and be comfortable with himself."

I took a look at the object of his intense curiosity and . . . it was a pretty cool dollhouse. It was a two-story colonial with a living room and a formal dining room. It had a winding staircase with a gold banister that led up to three bedrooms and two full baths.

Shit, it was nicer than my house. I wanted to move into it.

Next to the dollhouse were all of the little accessories. There was furniture, little pets, and packages of families. Two packages of families. One black. One white. Adam got really quiet.

We were back in the minivan headed home and Adam still hadn't said a word.

"So, you excited about your finger paints, buddy?" I asked. "You're gonna have a lot of fun with those."

"Yeah," Adam said, looking at his feet as they dangled loosely over the edge of his car seat. "Daddy, are you gonna get a dollhouse for Carolyn?"

Carolyn is my daughter. She was about two years old at the time.

"She's a little young, yet. When she's older, we'll see."

"If you do," he said, "can you get the white family and not the brown family?"

My brain froze. It was as if it were a hot day and I'd tried to drink a Slurpee a little too fast.

"The white family? Why?" I managed to sputter.

"Because," he said still gazing at his little blue Converse All Stars.

"Because why?"

"Because brown people are bad," he said.

We'd never talked about race before. Where the hell did this come from??

"Who told you that brown people were bad, son?" I asked.

"My friend Tommy; his daddy told him. Brown people are bad." He finally looked up from his shoes, catching my eyes in the rearview mirror. "Am I bad, Daddy?"

My eyes stung. They were watering.

"Of course not. You're a very good boy. I'm very proud of you," I whispered.

He got a slight look of relief on his face that quickly changed to concern.

"Are *you* bad, Daddy?"

How does a father answer a question like that?

"Not today." I smiled.

That was quick. Unfortunately not quick enough to ward off his anxiety.

"Daddy, I don't want to be brown! I don't want to be bad!" he yelled.

I had to throw up.

We got home and went into the house.

"Daddy, will you finger paint with me?" he asked.

"No, pal. Daddy doesn't feel well."

I ran upstairs to the bathroom and barely made it to the toilet before I puked my guts out. He was FOUR YEARS OLD FOR GOD'S SAKE. This kid Tommy was four, too. Is this where it starts? Is this how it starts?

"Daddy, will you finger paint with me now?" Adam said.

I felt the molasses engulfing me.

"No, pal. Daddy doesn't feel well."

"Honey, dinner's ready," my wife shouted.

"You guys go on ahead. I'm not hungry."

"Daddy, will you take me to school today?" Adam asked.

"No, pal. Your mom will take you. Daddy feels sad . . . I mean sick. Daddy feels sick."

CHAPTER 7

Pressure

"My opinion is that there is a kind of unconscious effort that has existed in the past to resist the integration of our community. How this is done, I can't really say. I can't put my finger on why this is true."

—Rev. Dorel Londagin, testimony before the U.S. Commission on Civil Rights Hearings, May 6, 1967

I stood in the kitchen listening to the voices through the receiver of the princess style phone. I had picked it up when it rang, not knowing it wasn't for me.

"I don't understand what you mean."

"It's simple. You have six people in your family. Six people are too many people for a three-bedroom apartment unit."

Mom was talking to Mr. Wentworth, the apartment manager.

"I don't see what the problem is. That's two people per bedroom."

"Well, that might be all right for a house, but our bedrooms are small, our units are small. You have too many people for these apartment units."

"Well," my mother continued, "you knew how large my family was when I filled out my rental application."

"Well, actually we didn't."

"It's right there on the rental application. Look at it."

"Well, that's just it, we can't seem to find your rental application."

There was a glacial pause.

"I'm sure you can't," she said, slamming down the phone and nearly deafening me in the process.

"Brian!" I heard her call from upstairs.

"Coming!"

I ran up the stairs and into her bedroom where I found her sitting on the corner of the bed. She had this look on her face. I'd seen it before.

A look that seemed to say, "I'm not going to lose control, because if I do . . . they win."

"Did you call me, Mom?"

"Are we the largest family you've seen in these apartments?" she asked.

"Let me think," I said, fidgeting with eight-year-old, Frosted Flakes–fueled energy. "Billy by the swimming pool lives with his mom, his dad, his three brothers, his aunt, his uncle, his cousins, and his grandparents, and the Ingalls have seven. Why?"

"No reason," she said. Her face took on the subtle assuredness of a poker player suddenly dealt the final card to fill an inside straight.

"Do me a favor," she said, handing me a crisp five-dollar bill. "Go to the store for me. Bring me back a Hershey bar with almonds and a *True Story* magazine. You can get yourself some *Superman* comic books with the change."

Her favorite escape from the world, her primary method of unwinding, her version of two stiff martinis to loosen up, was to close her bedroom door with a Hershey bar with almonds and disappear into the salacious drama of *True Story* magazine.

I guess that there was something about reading "He said he loved me, but I didn't know he had wives in three other states!" that made her problems seem trivial.

I took the money and looked at her.

"Go on now," she said gently. "Close the door."

I went out into the hallway, closed the door, and stood there for a minute. For obvious reasons, I didn't really want to go back out there by myself again. I heard my mother pick up the phone and dial.

"Mr. Wentworth? This is Mrs. Copeland. I'm sorry. We must have been disconnected. Now, you were saying that our family is too large for these apartments? Well, the Whitney family and the Ingalls family are both larger than ours. Am I to assume that they are getting this same call from you today?"

She paused for a moment, listening.

"Well, they most certainly are."

Another beat.

"Well, I would suggest that you check with them then. Good-bye."

I heard her triumphantly slam down the phone.

CHAPTER 8

School Days

"When I was a member of the San Leandro School Board in the late sixties, early seventies, there was a man who lived across the street from San Leandro High School who used to call me every two weeks. He'd say, 'When are you going to do something about all those black kids going to the high school? They don't belong here.' I'd say that they live in the district so they are entitled to go to that school. 'No,' he'd say. 'I see them getting off of buses. They're coming here from Oakland.' I'd say, 'No, they're not. If they didn't live here, they wouldn't be attending that school.' 'Well,' he said, 'I've been counting them every day and there's no way that many black kids live around here. They're from Oakland.' He was actually looking out his window and counting the black students as they left the building every day."

—Mimi Wilson, former San Leandro School Board member,
former president of San Leandro Fair Housing

In September, I began the third grade at Lewelling School, which was located conveniently next door to our apartment complex. On my first day, I walked over with Tracie, who was starting the first grade, and then I reported to Miss Hubbard's classroom.

I walked into the classroom and it was nice. It was clean, just like everything else in that town. The blackboard was green and the teacher's name was written on the board in yellow chalk. The top of the wall was lined with a train of covered wagons, each adorned with a letter of the alphabet written in cursive in both upper- and lowercase. The room was filled with desks. They were double desks, each with two children's chairs.

I sat down at the desk closest to the door. A boy with light brown hair occupied the other chair.

"Hi," I said.

"Hi," he said as he got up, walked across the room, and sat next to another brown-haired boy.

I sat alone watching the other boys and girls file in. Most glanced in my direction as I smiled. Some walked in pairs and found desks with two spaces to accommodate their friendships. Others looked at me and then scanned the room for a seat. A seat anyplace but next to me.

Finally, a little girl sat next to me as there were no other seats left. She was pretty, sporting long blond hair that was tied into two braids spruced up with red ribbons. She never took her eyes off me. She was staring. It felt weird.

"Hi," I said.

"Can I touch your hair?" she finally asked.

"Uh . . . okay." How else do you answer a question like that?

She took her little hand, extended her index finger, and gently touched the top of my head.

"It feels weird," she said.

The other kids in nearby seats were watching now. The girl pinched a little of my hair with her thumb and forefinger and rubbed it between them.

"It's like a Brillo pad."

The other kids laughed as I felt another hand touch my head from behind. I turned, startled to see a little boy sticking his finger in my neatly trimmed afro.

"It is!" he shouted with a laugh. The other kids joined him in laughter.

Soon, there were what seemed like hundreds of hands rubbing, pulling, tweaking, and massaging my hair.

"Brillo head!" one of the boys yelled, as the kids laughed.

"It *does* feel like a Brillo pad!" another boy said with laughter.

My stomach felt queasy. I wanted to go home. I contemplated getting up and walking out the door, when I was literally saved by the bell. As it rang, the kids let go of my hair and scrambled to their seats. I put my head down on my desk as the teacher walked in. As she started her beginning-of-the-school-year drill, I heard one of the kids behind me whisper to his desk mate.

"Brillo head," he said with a snicker.

The boy next to him started to snicker as well. He tried to stifle it. The more he tried to keep from laughing, the more he laughed.

"Brillo head," the second boy repeated.

This time, the girls at the double desk next to them overheard and they, too, attempted to suppress their giggles. One of them buried her head in her arms on her desk to hide her laughter.

The teacher continued with her spiel, oblivious to the hilarity ensuing right in front of her. The laughter was contagious. Stifled chuckles spread around the room like raging wildfire.

I learned to hate my hair. White kids always wanted to touch it. Nobody in town wanted to cut it. It was like no other hair I saw on a regular basis. I lived with all women and my sisters had their own issues with their hair. When they were little, they used to put sweaters on their heads to pretend that their hair was loose and mobile like that of the white girls they saw every day. Later, Tracie would have my mother take her into Oakland to a stylist who gave her some type of permanent that relaxed the strands, allowing her to swing her hair back and forth with every move of her head. She called it getting her hair "blond." She thought that was what you called hair that could move.

Later, Delisa would ask for her hair to be "blond," too, so that she could be like the white girls. Her permanent didn't take though. Something happened that caused all of her hair to fall out. There was a bad reaction to the chemicals. Poor Delisa found that being bald was even worse than having "black" hair. The teasing she endured was relentless. Her self-esteem shattered in ways that I doubt are repaired to this day.

I, too, wanted hair like the white boys. I wanted to flip my hair out of my eyes and run my fingers through it. I wanted to stick out my lower lip and blow upward, breezing it off of my forehead when I was frustrated. I wanted their hair. I wanted hair that the other kids didn't ask to touch.

From childhood to adulthood, I tried everything for "normal" hair. I tried straightening it with a hot comb, the result being a stiff, slightly scorched mop that retreated back to its original texture within a day or so. I tried grease. Grandma took me to Oakland, the only place to buy anything resembling African-American hair products, where I bought Dixie Peach that I slathered on my follicles by the handful. It stayed down but I still couldn't move it. I couldn't blow it out of my face and I sure couldn't flip it.

When I was a teenager, I saw Smokey Robinson singing on television. He had these beautiful, shiny curls. Beautiful, shiny *mobile* curls. I went to an Oakland hair salon and got my first Geri Curl. It was curly all right. It moved. I could flip it out of my face. I had to. The grease and oil that had to be put on it daily in order for it to retain its form was profuse and disgusting. I had to stock up on spray bottles of oily "activator." Without a daily dose, I had a mop of straw on my head. To make matters worse, it stained everything my head touched. If I rested my head against a chair or leaned against the backseat of the car, there was a gross, oily smudge.

Grandma hated it and blamed Smokey Robinson. When I worked with Smokey for the first time, years later, Grandma said, "Tell his ass he owes me for pillowcases."

The upside to the Geri Curled hair was that at last, finally, white people stopped asking me to touch it. They didn't want that greasy shit all over their hands, either.

In my early twenties, I finally settled on a texturizer. This was a process of straightening made possible by a smelly chemical rubbed into the hair by a stylist. The longer it stayed on, the straighter the hair would become. The only problem was that it burned like hell. It's like covering your scalp with paper cuts and then soaking it in rubbing alcohol. The trick is standing the pain long enough to get the hair straight, but not so long that you literally develop open sores on your scalp.

It was painful, but it worked. It was a process created by black people, for black people, administered by black people. That being the case, it was dismaying that the criticism I received for my hair being straight came almost exclusively from black people.

"You trying to be white," they would write me after seeing me on television.

"Why are you ashamed of your natural hair, you Nat King Cole–looking motherfucker?" one letter read.

Not ashamed. Not really. I just wanted to flip it. Is that too much to ask?

"Brillo head," I heard someone behind me say again.

I wanted to go home. I didn't want to be there. I wanted to go back into my room where I could be safe and alone. I could feel my eyes welling with tears. No. I wouldn't cry. Not there. Not then. I was my mother's son.

"If I lose control, they win."

Somehow, I managed. I made it through the morning. Since it was the first day, it was only a half day. At lunchtime, I was free. As the bell rang, I walked out of the classroom and ran home. I ran as fast as I could. I was in a race, only I wasn't exactly sure who my opponent was. I didn't know if I was racing the kids, their taunts, my sadness, or my anger at being "different." I just knew that I had to run and I had to do it before I started to cry.

I made it to the apartment and zipped toward the stairs. My mother sat on the plastic-sealed couch, reading one of her *True Story* magazines.

"Hi, honey. How was your first . . . ," I heard her say as I tore up the stairs, went into my room, and closed the door. I sat on my bed "Indian style," my pillow in my lap. I laid my head against its soft fluffiness and rocked back and forth. Now it was okay. Now the tears could come. I was safe. I was alone. I was always alone. Everywhere I went then. There in my room, walking down the street, in that classroom full of kids, I was all alone.

"I'm all by myself," I muttered as I drifted off to sleep against the moist pillow.

———

My first day was indicative of my experience at Lewelling. School days were filled with loneliness, taunts, and isolation. Few called me Brian. "Brillo head" had become my nickname.

"Knock the shit out of them," Grandma would say.

I didn't want to fight. I wasn't athletic and the few fights I'd had in my life had all ended with me bleeding from the mouth and in tears. Things deteriorated at school until I didn't have a choice.

At recess, when the boys chose teams to play kickball, basketball, or soccer, initially I was one of the first boys picked. Their exposure to blacks had come primarily from watching Wilt Chamberlain, Hank Aaron, O.J. Simpson, and the like on television. It was their assumption that all blacks were good athletes. My ineptness soon became apparent. I couldn't hit. I couldn't kick. I couldn't throw. I couldn't make a basket. In football, I couldn't throw or catch a spiral.

The other boys learned these skills from their dads. I didn't have that luxury. Sylvester had once had a brief, fleeting feeling of fatherhood and took me to the park one Saturday. He wanted to throw the football around. He fired a bullet pass to me that hit me in the chest so hard that I hit the ground. After that, I was afraid of the ball. He'd throw it to me and I'd dodge it.

"You ain't worth a shit," he said, finally giving up in disgust. "Get your ass in the car."

I didn't like sports because I wasn't good at them. I liked reading. I liked my comic books and reading the *World Book Encyclopedia* for interesting facts. These were not things expected of a boy. They certainly weren't the traits expected of a black boy, at least not as far as the kids at school were concerned.

"What kind of colored kid are you?" one white boy asked as I wildly threw a basketball that sailed a mile past the backboard.

Once it became evident that I was lacking in the physical

activity department, that I was weak and uncoordinated, that I wasn't a threat, it was like blood in the water to sharks. It was open season on "Brillo head." I fought daily. I fought before school, I fought after school. I fought at recess.

I was a godsend to the boys who had previously been the targets of the school bullies. They no longer had to worry about their own safety because everybody was focused on me. In fact, some of the boys who had been the school "rejects" were able to fit in with the other kids by beating *me* up. The oppressed became the oppressors.

School officials soon took notice of the fact that I was fighting a lot so they called my mother in for a conference. They wanted to know what *my* problem was. Why I was in so many fights. As if it were my choice; as if I were the aggressor. I just wanted to make friends. To fit in. To be normal.

It was decided that it might be better if I didn't associate with the other kids outside of class. My mother came up with the brilliant idea that at recess I should just sit on the bench and read. The school officials agreed. I wasn't allowed to play. So, for the next semester, every day at recess and at lunch I'd sit on the bench, a book in my lap, and watch the other kids play basketball, kickball, and four square. Sometimes, I'd hold my book up to my face so that when I felt sad, listening to the others running and laughing, they wouldn't see me. This solution wasn't really a solution. Unless I could somehow be dipped in bleach, I was destined to be a social outcast. My mother saw how unhappy I was. She knew the situation wasn't good or improving. It was at this point that she got the bright idea to send me to the local Catholic school.

"The Catholic kids will be nicer," she said. "They're Christ-centered."

My mother had been raised in the black Baptist church like

Grandma and her mother before her and every other family member as far back as memory would allow. Grandma had grown up in the church, singing in the choir for over twenty years and revolving her life around church activities.

Grandma once told me that when she was a kid, all family life was centered around the Baptist church. Sundays would be spent in services, from morning until night, praying, testifying, and singing. They would break for the enormous meal that my great-grandmother would prepare in celebration of Sunday, and then return to the church for more worship. That was in Birmingham, but it continued in some fashion even after Grandma's family moved en masse (parents, brothers, sisters, and every other relative) from Birmingham to Akron in 1945.

I vaguely remember it being a shock when my mother came home from work one day and announced that she was converting to Catholicism. I didn't even know what "Catholicism" or "Catholic" meant. I thought that "converting" to it, whatever that was, involved having some kind of an operation. When she said that I was converting, too, I was terrified I'd have to go to the hospital and go under the knife.

I don't remember Grandma arguing or trying to talk her out of it. My mother was always coming home with some new interest or radical diversion from various aspects of her life. I remember Grandma simply replying with her customary, "Shit," when Mom broke the news. Other than that, she was fairly supportive. Grandma never became a Catholic, but she went to more masses than most Catholics I know.

My sisters and I were baptized at St. Sebastian's Church in Akron in 1968, shortly after my fourth birthday. I remember it well. I remember holding lighted candles for the first time in my life and being more fascinated with the flame than the Latin words the priest was speaking. A woman my mother had

met through her job at Ohio Edison was our godmother and
her son our godfather, as Tracie, Delisa, and I began the life-
long trek of indoctrination. If you think that the list of black
San Leandro residents was short, check out the list of black
Catholics.

St. Felicitas church and school are located one mile, door to
door, from the apartment complex we lived in. It was estab-
lished as the sole Catholic parish in the Washington Manor
area in 1953. Its mission, like those of most institutions of this
type, was to create a community that was faithfully infused with
Roman Catholic doctrine. Logic would dictate that Tracie, Delisa, and I would fit right in. We were, after all, Catholics. Sure,
we didn't know all of the rituals that those who had grown up in
the church from birth were accustomed to. We weren't regular
mass attendees, so we weren't sure when to kneel or stand or
brush our foreheads and chins and all of the other things in the
service that look like signals a catcher is sending a pitcher behind
the batter's back (am I praying or bunting here?), but we were
fast learners and we were of the same faith. It would be a common frame of reference, no matter how tenuous.

The problem with being dropped into a Catholic-school
situation is that, while the student population of a public school,
especially one located next door to an apartment building, is
transient, a parochial school's student body is incredibly stable.
At St. Felicitas, many of the families had been with the parish
since its inception. Being good Catholics who followed the
Vatican's teachings on the evil that was birth control, there
were families with eight, nine, and even ten kids, all of whom
were matriculating through the church's school. The kids
knew each other from birth. Their parents socialized together.
Their big brothers and sisters had studied with the same teach-
ers and played on the same sports teams. Tracie, Delisa, and

I were, for lack of a better word, interlopers. Black interlopers who had injected ourselves into their community. Their white community.

The beginning was rough. Very rough. As hard as it may be to believe, it was even tougher than it had been at Lewelling. I didn't think that it was possible at the time, but I was even more of an outsider. The kids had their inside jokes and their stories from the funny things that happened in first grade and the days of their first communions. They had been there their entire educational careers, while I was entering my seventh school.

I became even more isolated. When the great sports expectations were dashed at recess and P.E., I was once again an outcast. Luckily my teacher, Lisa Carrion—a twenty-one-year-old who was teaching her first class—recognized my plight almost instantly. She made an extra effort to include me in classroom projects, even inviting me to her home to help her grade the other kids' papers. I was just a little boy, but for the first time, here was a white person who treated me like, well, an adult. Almost like a peer. Grandma liked her, but she was always careful, always skeptical, as her life experience had taught her to be.

"You ain't that woman's equal," she'd say, especially when I referred to Mrs. Carrion as "Lisa," which she allowed me to do when I was helping her after school and on the weekends. "You ain't that woman's equal!"

She may have been right in an authority/subordinate type of way. After all, she was my teacher and she was an adult. The thing is that for the first time in my life, here was a grown-up who treated me like I was an equal. Here was a white person who didn't look at me as "the black boy" or "the colored kid," but as Brian. Her kindness made life bearable.

Almost. The fights continued, mostly after school now.

Few wanted to get into the trouble that came with fighting on the campus of a Catholic school, so you'd be "chosen out" for a physical altercation.

"After school!" Someone would challenge, for the most innocuous of alleged transgressions. When school let out, I would have no choice but to go to the appointed place and duke it out. I always lost. As I've stated, I wasn't a fighter. The more I lost, the more I was "chosen out." Mom was right. Things were different here. Here, the bullies and bigots wore uniforms. There was no one to help me. Not even the Sisters of St. Joseph, whose order ran the school. Especially not the sisters.

It was lunchtime and I was sitting by myself on one of the orange school benches when two boys walked up to me.

"Hey, burr head," one of them shouted in my direction.

I had been upgraded from "Brillo head" to "Burr head" here. Ah, the refinement of the parochial-school experience. I ignored them and buried my head in the comic book I was reading.

"You too good to talk to us, coon?"

Coon? Here was a new one. This place was really expanding my vocabulary. I continued to ignore them. They walked closer to me. Soon they were in my face.

"I'm talking to you," the larger of the boys said. He was a transfer from Lewelling, just like me. He was a year older and had been held back, thus making him the "king of the school."

"King of the school" was a designation given to the boy who had the reputation that implied that he could beat up anyone in the school. You rarely saw one of these kids actually fight, because the rep was good enough to scare off would-be contenders. Every once in a great while, somebody would want a legitimate shot at the title, declare the "after school" challenge and, if he won, which almost never happened, he'd be crowned the new "king."

Our "king" was one of those grade-school kids so developed he looked like he paid child support. He snatched my comic book out of my hand and ripped it in half. I looked him dead in the eye.

"Fuck you," I said. I don't know where that came from. It just came out. I said, "Fuck you." He heard, "Please kick my ass."

The two boys grabbed me by the arms and dragged me into the boys' bathroom to beat me up. I struggled, but I was not going to scream or cry for help. I wouldn't give them the satisfaction. I wouldn't lose control.

"They may beat me to a pulp," I thought, "but I won't let them win. I'll never let them win."

I was thrown against the bathroom wall just as I heard the bell ring. I watched as his majesty the king balled his hands into fists. As he was preparing to swing, the door opened. The boys' heads snapped toward the sound just as Sister Ermina walked in. Sister Ermina was the principal. She was older, as most of the nuns were, and she had a face that was reminiscent of a French bulldog. She never wore a habit. None of the sisters wore them there. It was weird. I thought that they had to. I'd grown up watching *The Flying Nun*. Not only did I expect them to wear habits, I expected them to soar in formation with pelicans.

"What's going on in here?" she demanded with the perpetual scowl that she wore on her face. There was always a scowl. She was a nun. Why did all of the nuns always look so unhappy? Is this what it means to give your life to God? Frowning all the time? Pissed off for no apparent reason?

"What's going on in here?" she screamed again.

Silence. It was stone cold.

"I said, 'What is going on here'?" she repeated.

I ran past the boys and over to her.

"They were going to beat me . . ."

I didn't get a chance to finish my sentence or my thought. A sharp blow to my left cheek stung me into silence.

"Shut up," she said. "Get to class."

"But . . ." I managed to get out, choking back tears. "They were going to . . ."

She raised her hand to slap me again.

"I said, 'Get to class'!"

The boys smiled as they filed past us with a polite, "Yes, sister."

I rubbed my cheek, each stroke easing a little of the soreness. I went back to class and slunk down in my seat. Here, not only did the kids beat me up, so did the principal.

I heard my mother's voice in my head.

"They're Christ-centered."

I didn't remember the Bible story where Jesus slapped the shit out of the black kid. I must have missed catechism that day.

Grandma picked me up from school in the Chevy, so I didn't have to fight on the way home that day. I'd already had my physical altercation for the afternoon. During the mile drive I was sullen, quiet.

"Boy, what's wrong with you?" Grandma asked.

"Nothing."

At home, it was obvious that something was wrong. I didn't have a good poker face. I never did. The interrogation began anew.

"What the matter?" Mom asked.

"Nothing," I said again. I was not spending another semester on the bench, watching the white kids play.

"I'm fine."

"No you're not. What's wrong?"

I looked at the floor. Silent.

"Honey, I know you. I carried you for nine months."

Why do mothers always play that card? You got laid, so here I am. Quit throwing it in my face.

"Honey," she said, "you were once a part of me. I know when something's wrong."

She tucked a curled index finger under my chin, lifting my head to look me in the eye. Her eyes were warm, soothing. There is something about looking your mother in the eye. You can't lie to her. There is some maternal power that comes from your mother's gaze. It's like sodium pentathol. You are compelled to tell the truth. I think that we could probably cut down the expenses of the criminal justice process by 90 percent if we let suspects' mothers do the initial interrogation. She'd look her kid in the eye and ask about the bank robbery and he'd spill his guts on the spot.

Finally, I broke down and told her everything. I told her about the boys and the bathroom and being slapped by the principal. My mother was appalled. She grabbed the phone, called the convent, and confronted Sister Ermina.

"Did you put your hands on my son today?" she demanded.

"No. Of course not," came the reply, which was so loud I could hear it through the receiver.

"You didn't slap him? You didn't hit him in the boys' bathroom?"

"No! I would never do anything like that to one of our students."

My mother hung up the phone and looked at me. Here a Catholic nun, a woman whose life was devoted to spreading the teachings of Christ, a woman who wore a wedding ring because she was, in effect, spiritually and symbolically "married" to God, had just called me a liar. What kind of a place was this? It was like the Bizzarro World in my *Superman* comics. Up is down. Down is up. Bad is good. Good is bad. The truth is a lie and lies are the truth.

"She says that she never touched you," Mom said.

"But she did. She slapped me. I swear. I SWEAR!" I screamed, tears running down my cheeks. I thought, "Does anybody in this stupid city tell the truth?"

Mom picked up the phone again and called Mrs. Carrion at home. Lisa had endeared herself to my mother by her kindness toward me.

"Sister Ermina came by my classroom," Lisa said, "and told me to keep better control of my kids. She said that there were some of my boys goofing around in the bathroom and she hit one of them."

My mother's face changed. It morphed into a combination of sorrow, anger, and disappointment as she slowly put the phone back on its cradle.

"I told you," I said. "I told you."

The cops lied about me. The nuns lied about me. Was I that bad a person?

Grandma, as usual, made no attempt to try and hide her disgust. She knew these people and she knew this place. The climate may have been a little milder, the drawl in their voices absent, but she'd known these people all of her life.

"I should go down there and slap *her* ass!"

"Suer!" Mom said, shocked.

"I ain't gonna sit here and let her beat on the boy."

"But you can't do that. You can't go beating up a nun!"

"Shit," Grandma said. "Nuns. They can't do nothing else, that's why they nuns!"

It was a long evening, before it was finally decided that nothing would be done. I should steer clear of the principal as best I could. I should steer clear of the bullies as best I could. This was my life now and I'd better get used to it. Steering clear. This place was a minefield. The mines were laid everywhere and I didn't know where they were or when they would explode. I might be walking down the street looking for the park, on the school playground, or in the restroom, and the enemy was everywhere. They wore uniforms, business suits, and sometimes even crucifixes around their necks. It was up to me to navigate the minefield and I had to do it alone. Mom and Grandma couldn't hold my hand. I was alone. All alone.

I went back to school the next day and gritted my teeth. I endured the taunts and the slurs. I kept to myself as best I could. My sisters and I were the only blacks and we were just going to have to live with that.

Thirty years later I would discover an interesting fact. There was another with our complexion, a woman. A very prominent woman. Her name was St. Felicitas. For all of the racism, the slurs, and the ethnic putdowns we endured; for all of the times that strangers in this largely Catholic area would yell "nigger" from their car windows as my sisters and I walked down the street; for all of the hoopla over families of color living in the Washington Manor district, the area's sole Catholic church was named after a black woman.

It turns out that St. Felicitas was a black slave who, along with her white mistress, was martyred for the faith—thus making her a candidate for sainthood. I attended St. Felicitas for four years and was never told this interesting piece of Catholic history. I'm virtually certain that the overwhelming majority of those worshipping in that parish at that time were not aware of the ethnic background of their patron saint. If they had been, I wonder if she would have been banished to the other side of the "invisible wall." Or maybe that was the secret to residing in San Leandro if you were black. All I needed to be respected, treated equally, and not terrorized and harassed based on my race, was to be canonized. Christ-centered indeed.

CHAPTER 9

Breaking Down

Monday morning, six A.M. to be exact. I was tooling up Highway 101 in my brand new sports car. A 1999 Mazda Miata. British racing green. Five speed. It was the most amazing car I'd ever driven. (Yeah, sheltered automotive life. Indulge me.) Driving it was surreal. It was like being in a video game. I just knew that if I smashed up, the words START OVER would magically appear.

It was a gorgeous morning. The sun was just breaking over the mountains. I was on my way into Mill Valley to do a live-television remote. I was one of the hosts of the morning show for the local Fox TV affiliate. It was kind of a Bay Area *Today* show and I did daily remotes, like celebrity interviews and goofy man-on-the-street shtick.

When I say "shtick," that's exactly what I mean. I created a segment called "I Want to See It," a throwback to the early days of television and *You Asked for It.* Viewers wrote in with outrageous stunts that they'd like to see me attempt on live television and I obliged. It was crazy things like jumping into the San Francisco Bay, bungee jumping, and having my legs waxed. I'm a fan of television's golden age, so I relished the spontaneity. It was fun, but at the same time somewhat disheartening.

While the viewers loved the segments, I didn't feel listened to or respected by management or by my producers. I had little to no say in what I did. When I didn't have a viewer dare or a celebrity interview, my morning consisted of accosting strangers on the street as they headed to work, trying to get them to sing songs or eat bizarre things. An inordinate amount of my time was spent (not by my choice) standing in front of San Francisco coffee shops, talking to white yuppies eating bagels. God forbid I did anything that showcased or interacted with people of color.

It was really a love/hate relationship. I loved the people I worked with, but I was dissatisfied with the job. I'm a comic and a writer and I had no outlet for these gifts. On the other hand, I'd spent years working the road as a comic and now I had children who needed their daddy at home. I had a mortgage and parochial school tuitions. All of the white man's burdens. The pay was decent and the perks were terrific, but I was incredibly dissatisfied. I'd become the Man in the Gray Flannel Suit. I used to be a rebel. Now I went into work wearing a tie and I was accountable to people who couldn't give a rat's ass what I thought or had to say. I was in a cage. It was a gilded cage, but a cage nonetheless.

I actually fell into the job accidentally. I started out by doing funny commentaries on the news once a week and then, upon noticing that the program had no weatherman, I jokingly said, "This show would be a hit if only you had a funny black weatherman." Two weeks later, I got a call from the executive producer that the station manager wanted to see me about my idea.

"What idea?" I said.

"Your idea about doing the weather," she replied.

"I was just kidding."

"Well, it's too late now. The boss wants to see you. You have a lunch date on Friday at noon."

The next thing you know, I'm a fucking weatherman. I knew absolutely nothing about the weather. This is not necessarily a bad thing in the San Francisco area. Either it's going to rain or it's not. I could handle that. What I couldn't handle was my entire identity now revolving around temperature highs and lows. Here I had spent my adult life writing and establishing myself as a comic who did what no other black comics working clubs were doing—topical and political humor—and suddenly, all anybody wants to talk to me about is whether or not it's going to rain when they have their family picnic on Saturday.

I developed a following and I loved the production staff, crew, and my on-air coworkers, but I despised every minute of the job. Especially once black viewers began to write in with the same old challenges to my ethnic legitimacy. When you turn on your television in the mornings, with rare exceptions, you see black men only as the jolly, nonthreatening forecaster—Spencer Christian, Al Roker, Mark McEwan, etc. It has almost become a racist stereotype. Apparently, that's all America can accept from a black man in the morning, advice on whether or not to send your kids to school in a sweater. I was accused of being every kind of Uncle Tom, simply because I had a job on television, a medium I've adored my entire life.

As I wrote earlier, I'm a radio-talk-show host and had been for a few years prior to getting the morning-show job. I had interviewed everybody from politicians to celebrities to criminal defendants in high-profile cases to any and every imaginable newsmaker. Talk radio was great. I wanted more from television. It was only when I threatened to quit and actually walked out of my TV general manager's office that I was promoted to the cohost job that I now held. Still, the meaty stuff for TV was off-limits. On the radio I could talk to the governor about budget cuts. On TV, I was expected to dress like an Elvis impersonator as I spent a morning watching them prepare for their annual convention.

The best thing I got from this television experience was that for the first time in my life, I felt accepted. Having strangers walk up to me in the store and say hello made me feel "normal." Like a real person. It was funny to run into some of my childhood tormentors, now grown men, who would puff up their chests as they introduced me to their wives and kids while they bragged about how we grew up together. No mention was ever made of the beatings or the epithets. I was just one of the guys when we were kids. The boob tube had finally given me what I'd longed for since childhood. I was accepted and I belonged.

As much as I hated the job, the day I drove the Miata to work was a good day. I was going to do a few segments interviewing one of my childhood heroes, James Doohan—Scotty from *Star Trek*. I've been a *Star Trek* fanatic since I was ten years old.

Is that black? Well, they do have black Vulcans now. How does *that* work?

Do they make the Vulcan peace sign while stoically intoning, "That is illogical, motherfucker"?

I met James Doohan once. I was twelve and at my first *Star Trek* convention. After waiting in the autograph line for hours, I finally got up to the table and thrust my hand out for him to shake. He grasped it firmly, and I noticed something didn't feel quite right. *It wasn't all there. He was missing the middle finger of his right hand!!*

I didn't remember that episode:

CAPTAIN KIRK: *Mr. Scott, I've got to have five fingers.*
SCOTTY: *Sorry, Captain, but four's all there be!*

It's kind of a disquieting thing to shake hands with a digit amputee when you're not expecting it. It's like talking to somebody with a lazy eye. You never know which eye you're supposed to be looking at during the conversation. Guess that's why I never made it a point to meet Marty Feldman and Jack Elam.

With the aid of the wonder that is the Internet, I later learned that Doohan had landed on Juno Beach on D-Day as a member of the Royal Canadian Artillery (yes, the world's most famous Scotsman was actually Canadian). While walking across a minefield, his unit came under machine gun attack from the Germans. Doohan took four bullets to his leg and had his finger blown off.

Note to self: *Don't freak out when you shake his hand.*

The air was crisp that morning. There was an orange hue to the sky. Life was good. No, life was great. I was in my new sportscar. It was a gorgeous morning and I got to spend a few hours with one of my childhood heroes. I didn't think I could have planned things any better than this.

As I was savoring my good fortune, I started to feel like my breath wasn't quite filling my lungs. The following breath extracted a little less air, as did the next. My chest was tightening. It felt like somebody had violently grabbed me by the front of my shirt, balled it up, and twisted it in their burly fist, only instead of my shirt, they had the muscle and tissue of my chest.

Now my vision was blurry. It was as though I were looking through the lens of a camera that had been smeared with Vaseline to hide the wrinkles an aging model didn't want captured for posterity. After a minute or so, I realized that my vision wasn't blurry. The blur was from the tears. They were streaming down my cheeks.

I pulled over to the shoulder of the road and put the car in neutral. I made it just in time before I lost all power over my body. I began to convulse violently. I was sobbing uncontrollably.

"Why? *Why?*" I screamed as I pounded my new dashboard with my fist. "What the hell's wrong with me?"

CHAPTER 10

Just Like a Normal Boy

"San Leandro has its share of hypocrites like anywhere else. For example, the San Leandro Boys' Club's membership is 30 percent black because many blacks find the East Oakland Boys' Club lacking good facilities. As a result of the increase in black members, many white parents are holding back their financial support of the club. It takes fifty dollars to support the activities of each boy.

"One local merchant who is withholding his financial support told me, 'I have to sell to them, blacks, but I don't have to support them.' That's outright bigotry."

—San Leandro mayor Jack Maltester, November 1969

In my quest (and my mother's) for me to become a "normal, red-blooded, all-American boy," I joined the Boy Scouts. I enjoyed the club because a lot of it was about goal-setting. The achievement of these goals was measured by the acquisition and accumulation of merit badges. In order to get a merit badge in a particular area, a scout had to complete a set of criteria under the guidance of a counselor certified by the Boy Scouts of America in that specific badge.

After I'd received a dozen or so merit badges in camping, hiking, cooking, first aid, and the like, I set my sights on a badge in fishing. I'd always liked fishing, although I didn't know much about it and had never actually caught a fish. Sylvester, in a rare moment of fatherly impulse, had taken me out once when I was about six. I recall very little of the trip. I remember sitting in the backseat of a big 1968 Chrysler Imperial, which was packed with his adult male friends; genuine black men. I watched in confusion as they rolled and passed cigarettes between them, back and forth in front of my face. The smoke smelled odd to me, not like cigarette smoke I'd smelled before. I remember giggling hysterically for no apparent reason, getting really hungry, and then waking up hours later in my bedroom. I don't think I even got to see the water.

I checked with my scoutmaster and got the name of the local fishing counselor. He was the owner of one of the oldest real estate firms in San Leandro, the business having been in the family for generations. I called him, told him what I was hoping to accomplish, and we had a nice conversation. He told me about his commitment to scouting and how he would show me all of the ins and outs of fishing. He'd take me up to Lake Chabot, our local fishing spot, teach me about tackle, how to tie the appropriate knots for various hooks and lures, and the different techniques required for catching different types of fish. I was thrilled. I'd finally get to go fishing!

When he was certain that I'd mastered all of the fundamental techniques and required nuances of the sport, he'd sign my blue card indicating that I'd earned, and was to be awarded, the merit badge. We made an appointment for me to come into his real estate office for an initial meeting and to lay out our plan for achieving the requirements.

"You sound like a bright, well-mannered young man," he said. "I look forward to meeting you."

I was in the backseat of the Malibu as Grandma drove toward downtown. Mom sat in the passenger seat going over some papers from her office. She was a secretary for one of the big defense contractors located in San Francisco and she often brought her typing home to do at night and on the weekends. She needed to make copies of some of the documents and there was a place with a copy machine not far from the real estate office where I was meeting the fishing counselor.

"I can't wait to go fishing," I said.

"You know I ain't gonna clean 'em," Grandma said. "I'll cook 'em for you, but you gonna have to clean and scale 'em yourself."

"I don't know how to do that."

"I'm sure your counselor will teach you," Mom said without looking up from her papers.

"Yeah, I think it's one of the requirements for getting the badge."

We arrived at the real estate office and I got out.

"How long you gonna be?"

"I don't know, Grandma. He didn't say. Probably a little while."

"Okay, we'll go do what we got to do and then come back and wait in the car. I'll be parked right here," she said.

I walked into the outer office. It was small and there were few desks, all of which were occupied. There was the familiar chatter of a work environment. There was also a sudden, familiar silence as I walked in. A white woman behind one of the desks looked startled as I entered.

"May I help you?" she said.

"I'm here to see Mr. Richards."

"May I ask what this is regarding?"

"The fishing merit badge. My name is Brian Copeland. We talked on the phone. I have an appointment."

She looked down at an appointment calendar on her desk.

"Just a minute," she said.

She got up and walked into one of the adjoining offices. A minute later, a tall thin man with graying hair walked out abruptly. He extended his hand and smiled.

"Brian?"

"Yes, sir."

"I'm Mr. Richards. Did you bring your merit-badge card with you?"

"Yes."

"May I see it please?"

I took out the blue card and handed it to him. He took the card, pulled out a pen from his vest pocket, put the card on one of the desks, and quickly wrote on it.

"Here you go," he said, handing the card back to me.

I took the card back. The line that the counselor signs upon completion of the requirements was signed.

"You're all set," he said as he put his arm around my shoulder and led me to the door. He said a final, "Good luck to you," as he ushered me out.

I was in and out in less than five minutes. I stood on the street corner staring at the card in my hand. I didn't get it. I was pondering the experience as Grandma pulled up in the Malibu. She stopped and I got in.

"Wasn't he in?" my mother asked.

"Yeah, he was in."

"That sure was a quick meeting. When are you going fishing?"

"I don't know. He signed my card to get the badge."

"He signed your card?" she gasped. "But, you haven't done anything yet."

"I know. He signed it and said I was all set."

There was a silence in the car. A long silence. I could feel my mother fuming. Finally, as always, Grandma broke the impasse.

"He didn't know you was black."

My mother looked at her lap.

I wondered if her mind had just taken the same trip back in time that mine had. To Killeen, Texas, just a few short years before. Sylvester was stationed at Ft. Hood and we moved from Akron to join him. When we got to Texas, we stayed on the base in temporary housing while my mom tried to find us a house. I have vivid memories of playing with my Hot Wheels at my mother's feet while she was on the phone. I could only hear her side of the conversation.

"So it's four bedrooms? And it's close to a good school . . . That's sounds wonderful . . . Yes, I can be there tomorrow . . . Three o'clock at your office? Fine . . . One last thing. My family is black, will that be a prob . . . Oh . . . I see . . . Well, thank you anyway."

Over and over again. The same conversation, the hopeful, optimistic tone in her voice being suddenly dashed. Her dreams deflating like a tire that's been punctured by a rusty nail.

"Carolyn sounds like she's white on the phone," Grandma later explained. "She went to look at a house there and it got nasty when the folks saw that her skin didn't match her voice."

I thought of how, last Christmas, she called the department store and used an English accent when she asked them to increase her credit for the holidays.

"I need more pounds . . . oops . . . I mean dollars, luv!" she had said. She got her extra credit.

I guessed I sounded "white," too. Did this mean that I had to have the Texas conversation?

"Yes . . . the fishing merit badge sounds fun . . . Sure I can go to the lake . . . I'd love to learn how to bait a hook . . .

Monday at five? Sure . . . Oh, by the way, I'm black, is that . . . I see. Thanks anyway."

With moist eyes, Mom craned her head and peered at me around her seat.

"I'll take you fishing, honey."

CHAPTER 11

The Other Foot

For weeks after my thirty-fifth birthday party, I was restless. Nothing was fun anymore. I had a two-foot-high stack of comics next to my bed. I went to the comic book store dutifully each Wednesday when the new books arrived. I'd pay for them, bring them home, and then sit them in the pile. I didn't read them. I just didn't feel like it. I'd kept up on the adventures of my colorful heroes since I was seven, but I just hadn't been into it lately. I couldn't seem to get into anything at all.

Maybe I was just tired. I had been working seven-day weeks for most of the previous five years. I'd get up at 3:30 and drive to my location for the morning show, then I'd either go to the station to prepare for the following day's show or I'd do it at home. After that, I might nap for an hour or so and then get to work preparing my radio show. Next I'd read my customary seven newspapers and try to write some jokes for the stage and a television commentary for the noon news program at the station. Once that was done, I'd shower, get dressed, and go to a stand-up gig. After the show, I'd drag myself home at about midnight. I'd be exhausted, but too keyed up to sleep so I'd make myself a martini. After I drank it and showered, I'd climb into bed at around one. In two and a half hours, it would start all over again. Even though we lived in the same house, my wife and kids became passing acquaintances.

Some weeks were more challenging than others. I'd been doing a lot of work with Aretha Franklin's band of late. She played Atlantic City quite frequently and I'd open the show. On those occasions, I'd catch a flight from Oakland to Philadelphia on Friday morning right after signing off the TV program. Upon landing in Philly, the casino we were playing would send a car that took me on the hour-and-a-half ride to Atlantic City, where I barely had time to shower, shave, change, and make the sound check. I'd eat a little something, maybe nap for an hour, and then I'd do the show. After the show, I'd work on writing jokes and commentaries in my room until I dropped off to sleep. This pattern continued through Sunday night when I'd run offstage to a waiting car that already had my luggage loaded. It would shuttle me the hour and a half back to Philly where I would catch the red-eye back to Oakland. I'd land in Oakland at around three or three-thirty in the morning, catch a cab home, shower, shave, and then run out the door to my morning-show location where I'd have to be on the air at 6:45.

Five years of this. I was wound up like a drum, but I didn't know what to do about it. My agency was sending me offers for engagements and a local Realtor I knew had some good deals on some investment property he thought I should look at. I hadn't responded to either overture. I couldn't decide. I was having trouble making up my mind. I couldn't seem to decide the simplest things. I'd been driving poor waitresses crazy by changing dinner orders two and three times before settling on something. My focus was not as sharp as it normally was, either. I was spending more and more time looking for car keys that were already in my hand.

I always felt like I was on the verge of coming down with something. I was achy and dizzy a lot. My doctor said that

I needed more exercise. He thought that it would relieve some of the stress and help keep my weight, which was starting to creep up on me for the first time in my life, in check. On his orders, I started running again. I had loved running. I did it for ages. I ran 10k races and I even finished the San Francisco Marathon, but in recent years, who had the time? I had to do something, though, so I made it a point to try and make the time to run at least a few miles every day.

It was a beautiful morning as I walked out the front door, dressed for my run. The sky was clear. The sun was shining. There was a slight chill to the air. It wasn't cold; just cool enough so that a good run would bring my body up to a comfortable temperature. For me, that's the point in my run where I'm just "misty"—not dripping with sweat, just a little moist all over. I love that feeling.

As I walked down the street to warm up, I saw a car I'd never seen in the neighborhood before. It was an older sedan, a little beaten up, with dents and oxidized paint all over the body. The car was parked along the curb about a block from my house. As I approached, I saw its occupants: two young black men in their twenties. One sat in the driver's seat, the other in the backseat. This was weird. I didn't recognize them. There weren't many black people who lived in my neighborhood. I only knew of an older black couple who lived about a mile up the road.

As I walked by, the brothers looked at me, smiled, and waved. Nervously, I waved back. Why was I nervous? It was just two guys sitting in a car. I didn't know why, but I just felt funny about them. My spider senses were tingling. What were these two guys doing here? This little Jiminy Cricket–like voice went off in my head.

"You mean, 'what are these two *black* guys doing here,' don't you?" it said. "Just because they're black men, you're suspicious of them."

"No . . . no, I'm not. Really," I argued. "They're just out of place here."

"Out of place, my ass," Jiminy said. "You don't like seeing niggers in your neighborhood. You're just as prejudiced as the white people."

Was he right? No. He couldn't be. I'd been on the other side. I'd dealt with this stuff all my life. I tried to rationalize with him.

"C'mon, people don't just sit in their cars in this neighborhood."

"You mean *black* people don't just sit in their cars in this neighborhood. They could be here for a million reasons. Maybe they're picking somebody up. Maybe their car broke down and they're waiting for Triple-A. Maybe they're here selling Mary Kay products, for all you know. You're a racist bigot!"

That's impossible. I couldn't be. Could I? No. He was wrong. This was suspicious. Or was it? Would I have the same feeling if it were two white guys sitting in their car? Would I wonder what they were doing there? Or would I just assume that they were visiting some of their white friends in my white neighborhood?

I remember Jesse Jackson saying once that when he walked down the street at night and heard fast-approaching footsteps, he was relieved when it turned out that they belonged to white men instead of black. That's a big change for a black man who marched with Martin Luther King Jr. and fought Jim Crow in the South. When he was a kid, it was the white footsteps charging behind you in the middle of the night that you had to worry about.

Was I doing the same thing? Had I been so brainwashed by white society, so indoctrinated by the negative images I had seen in the media, so influenced by the barrage of pictures and news footage of black men in handcuffs and on wanted posters that I had become one of "them"?

I've got to be honest and admit that I've had Jesse's experience, walking down a dark street. If even I fear black men, what right do I have to be upset when white people fear and prejudge me? These guys were *just sitting there.* They were minding their own business. I should mind mine.

I took off on my run. I was so consumed by guilt that I barely noticed the five miles at all. I was running on autopilot. I was in a hypnotic haze. Was I now my own worst enemy? Had I become the very people who had hurt me the most?

"White-washed!" Jiminy said in my ear.

Forty-five minutes later, I finished running and began walking the same path I had walked for my warm-up. I saw the sedan. They were still parked there. They were still sitting in the same positions; one in the front seat, the other in the back. Jiminy sensed my apprehension and wouldn't let up.

"Go ahead, bigot. Why don't you call the police? *Help! Help! There are* niggers *in the neighborhood without a permit!*"

I tried to reason with him again.

"Come on, man. This is weird. They don't live here."

"Yeah," he said, "and black people should *never* be in any neighborhood they don't live in. Fuck freedom of association and all that shit. You're right. They shouldn't be here. Neither should an eight-year-old black boy carrying a baseball bat to the park."

Ouch. His words stopped me dead in my tracks as I turned around and looked at the car from the rear. I saw from the lettering on the back of the vehicle that it was an Oldsmobile Cutlass. No license plate.

"This is different," I muttered.

"Yeah. This time, *you're* the bigoted fuck."

"They've been sitting here for a long time. Who sits in a car for forty-five minutes? It's weird, and I *am* the head of the neighborhood watch."

"The neighborhood watch? You are just mister white up-standing citizen, aren't you? You want to call the cops on them?" he said in my ear with disgust. "You want to turn them in? Go ahead. Call the cops to come hassle them for having the nerve to sit in a car on your block. Your *white* block. But, if you do, don't *ever* complain again about white people jumping to conclusions about your black ass. Call the police. Go ahead. While you're at it, I saw a Mexican walking down the street without a leaf blower. Turn his ass in, too!"

I walked around for another twenty minutes pondering what, if anything, I should do.

"Okay, I'm gonna walk around and cool off for another half mile. If they're still here when I get back, I'll call the cops. Two guys sitting in a car that long is probable cause."

"Yeah," Jiminy said. "Probably *'cause* they're black. You're an asshole."

I walked around for another half mile and then headed back toward home. They were still sitting there. I was still rationalizing.

"This isn't right. There's one in the front seat and one in the backseat."

"Oh," Jiminy said, "so I guess black people can't have chauffeurs?"

"Fuck this!" I spat.

I went into the house, grabbed the phone book, and looked

up the nonemergency number for the San Leandro Police Department. Jiminy was still on my ass.

"No, call 911. There are niggers on the block in your lily-white neighborhood. This is an emergency. Tell them to send SWAT and the National Guard!"

I dialed the nonemergency number and the operator answered.

"San Leandro Police Department."

"Uh, yes . . . Hi . . . this is probably nothing . . ." I let out a nervous laugh. "I'm sure it's nothing . . . well, there are these two guys sitting in a car on my street and they've been there a long time and . . ."

"Tell her they're niggers and she'll send a squad car," Jiminy said.

"Shut up!" I yelled. Enough was enough.

"Excuse me?" the operator said.

"Look, I'm sure it's nothing, but there are these two guys who've been sitting in a car on my block for over an hour. I think it's odd because people don't usually sit and park on my street."

Then, she asked the $64,000 question.

"What do they look like?"

"What do they look like? Well . . . they're young. I'd guess late teens or early twenties." I quickly mumbled the words, "They're black," before returning to a clear and intelligible, "and they're in a beat-up, old white Oldsmobile Cutlass."

"I'm sorry," she said. "What did you say their race was again?"

I paused for a moment. It was a long moment.

"They're black. African American." There, I said it.

"I see," she said. I could hear the clickity clack of her fingers furiously tapping on a computer keyboard.

"See?" Jiminy said. "She's gonna send a squad car."

"I'm gonna send a squad car," she said. "Where exactly are they parked?"

I could hear Jiminy chuckle.

I gave her the precise street corner.

"They're parked on the right-hand side of the street."

She asked for, and I gave her, my name and address.

"We'll check it out right away," I heard her say as I mumbled a thank-you and hung up the phone.

"Happy?" Jiminy sneered.

I could hear him mocking me relentlessly.

"You are so much better than them, aren't you?"

"No. I'm not. I'm just watching out for my neighbors, that's all."

"For your white neighbors, you mean."

He laughed.

"Remember," he said, *"you're still a nigger."*

I hung my head at my chest. I really felt shitty. Had I just racially profiled? To white America, the face of crime is young, black, and male. I'd just bought right into it. Would I have called the police on the young black boy walking to the park with his bat and ball? What in the world had happened to me? The oppressed had now become the oppressor.

As night fell, there was a knock at my front door. I opened it to find two San Leandro cops standing there. My heart leaped into my throat. There are certain things that elicit that response for me. One is when I sit on the butcher paper on the examination table in the doctor's office (too many bad memories of childhood inoculations, I guess); the others are flashing red and blue lights in my rearview mirror, and two cops standing at my front door.

"Mr. Copeland?" one of the cops said.

I loved how they called me "Mr. Copeland" now.

"Yes?"

"We understand that you made a call to the department this morning regarding a strange vehicle in the area."

Oh shit. They were gonna give me hell for wasting the valuable time and resources of the San Leandro Police Department on a frivolous call.

"Yes . . . Look, I said that it was probably nothing when I called. I didn't mean to waste anybody's time."

"No," the other cop said, "you don't understand. The house they were parked in front of was burglarized."

My jaw dropped.

"What?"

"We're pretty familiar with their M.O. because they've been operating in this neighborhood for a few weeks now. The guy in the front seat is the driver and lookout. The one in the back is there to help the third with the heavy lifting."

"Third? There was no third."

"You didn't see him because he was in the house looting it."

The first cop spoke up again.

"They work in teams of three. The guy in the house pulls all of the cases off of the pillows and then fills them with as much loot as he can grab before he figures his time is up and he'd better get out of there. Kind of like a burglar's shopping spree."

Did he just say "loot"? I've never heard anybody say that in real life before. I smiled.

Well, Jiminy, what do you have to say about that?

He was surprisingly quiet.

I asked the policemen, "Did you catch them?"

"No, by the time we got a squad car down here, they were gone."

It was my fault that they had gotten away. If I'd called the police when I first thought about it, they would have been cooling their heels in a cell at that moment instead of scoping out the next house to rob. Maybe mine.

"We were hoping that maybe you could give us a better description," he said.

"How?" I thought. They were young brothers.

"Yeah," Jiminy said, "and they all look alike."

"Shut the fuck up!" I yelled.

The cops looked at me.

"Sorry. Not you guys."

I told them all I could about the car, its dents and lack of a license plate. My description of the burglars was vague. They were just two young black men. That's all I could tell them. I didn't know how tall they were—they were sitting down. There was nothing distinctive about their haircuts or clothing that I could see. The cops thanked me and were on their way.

I felt terrible, sick to my stomach. I didn't understand it. I should have been jumping up and down with glee because I was right. My suspicions were validated. They *were* crooks. They were indeed up to no good. Calling the police was the right thing to do. I guess that's why I felt so bad.

Calling the police *was* the right thing to do. Seeing two black men parked in my neighborhood meant that they were up to something. Did this mean that all of the times that I was stopped walking down the street, going for my run, or just driving along, minding my own business, the police were justified?

Now I was angry. I try so hard to live a good life. I try so hard to be a good person, husband, father, and citizen and all of that can be erased and painted with a brush of suspicion because of the actions of two black men I didn't even know. What they do makes *me* look guilty in the eyes of the police and of white America.

I thought of all of the times that I watched the news or read the paper and learned of some horrific crime. I thought of the times that I learned about senseless violence, rapes and murders, carjackings and abductions, robberies and burglaries. I thought of how my first reaction was always, "Please, God, don't let it be a black man. Please let the suspect be white." Most times, I was disappointed. I was disappointed and I was angry because nearly every time it *was* a black man and it made *my* life harder. It made it that much easier to believe the worst about me. It made it simpler to overlook my accomplishments and attempts to make positive contributions to society. It gave aid and comfort to the prejudiced and the bigoted. It gave them the smug confidence to say, "See how *they* are?"

Yet, I was being told that *I'm* not a "real" black man.

I wished I hadn't called the police. I wished that I hadn't been informed of what they were up to. I was sick and I was sad and I just wanted to hide away and do what I should have done that morning: mind my own business. The problem was that anything negative or derogatory that black people do *is* my business because, like it or not, I'm stuck with the social ramifications of it.

"I can't win. I can't win," the refrain went over and over in my head. "No matter what I do, I can't win."

"No, you can't," Jiminy said. "Why don't you know that by now?"

CHAPTER 12

Leakfast

"When the black people improve themselves economically, then they become more accustomed to the white man's ways and more desirous of becoming a part of it."

"Becoming a part of the white man's ways?"

"Well, you know, the white man's culture."

"Do you know any blacks who have said this?"

"No."

—Interview with Frank King, executive vice president
of the San Leandro Chamber of Commerce, November, 1971

ooking back on it from a perspective of thirty-five years,
my mother worked very hard at learning "the white man's
culture," from the books she read (all of the best-sellers
among white women of the day, *Fear of Flying*, *The Stepford
Wives*, *The Reincarnation of Peter Proud*, *Looking for Mr. Goodbar*)
to her conversion to Catholicism, to her switch to the Republican party. She tried to assimilate in any and every way possible.
Her unspoken philosophy was that while we may not look like
them, we could sure as hell act like them if that's what it took
to be accepted; if that was what we had to do to succeed.

———————

It was Sunday morning and we were pulling out of the parking lot of St. Felicitas Church where I had just served my first mass as an altar boy. It was fun and it made my mother happy.

I was in the backseat with my sisters. Grandma was driving. Mom, as usual, sat in the passenger seat. She never learned how to drive; she was always too nervous.

"I'm very proud of you, Brian," she said, craning her neck around her seat in order to make eye contact. "You looked very handsome in your robes."

I smiled. It made me happy to please her.

"I liked it. At communion, I got to hold the little catcher thing under people's chins in case they dropped the bread. A couple of times old ladies came up who couldn't get their tongues out for Father to put the bread on . . . so I jabbed them in the neck with the catcher thing to make their tongues stick out farther!" I said, proud of my ingenuity.

"Brian!!!" she shrieked.

Whoops. Maybe it wasn't that ingenious.

"Well, Father had to put the bread on it, Mom."

Grandma shook her head.

"Now them doggone white folks gonna be sayin' you hit 'em in church."

Grandma was paranoid. She was always looking ahead to what white people might accuse us of. When she would start to go off like that I would say, "Come on, Grandma. This isn't Birmingham. This is Northern California. This is the 1970s."

But Grandma was paranoid. Take Halloween. We were allowed to go trick-or-treating until Grandma said, "Some white folks might say y'all was involved in some devilment. If you here with us, they can't say you did nothing."

That was the end of trick-or-treating, but we still got to

give out candy. For a while, anyway. Then Grandma said, "Some white folks might get some mess in they candy and say it came from the niggers' house. If we ain't giving nothing out, they can't say we did nothing."

My mother said, "That's okay. We can have a party here. You can give each other candy."

She always tried to straddle that fence between making us fit into that indefinable box that she considered "normal" and compensating for situations when the realities of the social climate made it impossible to fit our square pegs into the round holes of that box.

"Well," she said, dismissing my transgression at communion, "I'm very proud of you, and we're going to go celebrate."

"We are?"

"Yes we are," she said. "We're going to brunch."

"What's brunch?" Tracie lisped, the effects of her thumb-sucking addiction becoming more evident with each syllable.

My mother smiled. "It's what you have when it's too late for breakfast and too early for lunch."

Under her breath, Grandma muttered a disgusted, "White folks shit."

"Do you mind?" Mom snapped in that clipped way of speaking that she used to express displeasure.

In hindsight, I don't know if my mother really was impatient with Grandma's cussing or if she just hated being called on her bullshit.

So, we drove into nearby Hayward for our first brunch and pulled into the parking lot of the fanciest breakfast place in town: the International House of Pancakes. We walked into IHOP dressed to the nines in our Sunday best.

After a short wait, this little bleached-blond waitress (with prominent dark roots) came over to show us to our table. I guess that I can best describe her attitude as—well, perhaps "resigned" is the right word.

"Come on, follow me," she said without making eye contact. She spoke in that breathy, "I don't really want to be bothered by you" tone that hormonal adolescent girls use when their parents have the unmitigated gall to ask them how school was that day.

We took her direction and squeezed into two bright orange booths sandwiching a faux-wood-grained table.

Wow, look at all the syrup.

Tracie, as always, had to be the shit disturber.

"Mommy?"

"Yes, honey?"

"Instead of 'brunch,' why don't they call it 'leakfast'?"

Kids. Naively logical.

My mother searched in vain for a logical answer. There wasn't one.

"Because . . . because . . . put your napkin in your lap, honey. Brian, take your elbows off of the table."

"So," I asked, "what do you eat for 'brunch'?"

"I'm going to have the cheese blintzes," she said.

"Shit," Grandma said. "I want me some grits and some eggs."

Poor Tracie and I looked back and forth at each other. We didn't know what to do. Grandma was cussing. Mom was ordering frou-frou food. I was overwhelmed looking at three or four hundred different kinds of syrup.

"Okay, I'll have the cheese blintzes, too," I said, ever the good son. Always the people pleaser. "What are they?"

It worked. The smile in her eyes told me that she was delighted. She had that rare gift, the ability to smile with her eyes.

"They're crepes filled with cream cheese and strawberry preserves."

"White folks shit," Grandma hissed.

I could feel the heat from the dirty look my mother gave her. Tracie saved her.

"Can I just have syrup?"

"No," Mom cut her off.

"Okay," she said, disappointed. "Shit."

There are few things on this earth funnier than somebody cussing with a lisp. "Shit" comes out sounding like "thit." I bit my lower lip to stifle my laughter. My mother was shocked.

"What did you just say?"

"Shoot. I said 'shoot.'"

Grandma smiled.

The waitress came over to take our order. She still avoided eye contact.

"Okay, what'll it be?"

I have always hated feeling that my mere physical presence was somehow an imposition.

She came back later and flung our food on the table.

"Okay, will there be anything else?" she said, in a way that translated to "Now will you just leave me alone?"

"That will be all. Thank you," Mom said, her politeness tinged with frost.

Tracie reached for a fork and my mother slapped her hand. The smack was loud enough to turn the heads at the neighboring tables.

"Tracie, where does your napkin belong?"

Tracie put her napkin in her lap, I followed suit, and we looked at my mother before we dared dream of touching a utensil.

"Grace first," my mother said.

We crossed ourselves, bowed our heads, and said in unison:

"Bless us, oh Lord, and these Thy gifts that we are about to receive, from thy bounty through Christ our Lord. Amen."

It was looking as though we'd finally get to eat in peace until Tracie, again, had to open her mouth.

"How come Grandma didn't say grace?"

"Because I ain't Catholic," Grandma said, raising a scrambled egg–covered fork to her lips.

"Come on Suer . . ." Mom pleaded.

We looked at Grandma in anticipation. Work with her, Grandma.

She forcefully placed her fork on her plate, folded her hands in reverence, and bowed her head.

"Thou shalt not steal."

"That's *not* grace!" my mother hissed through clinched teeth.

"It's in the Bible," Grandma said, defiant, retrieving her forkful of eggs.

"But it's not a blessing. It's not grace."

"If it was good enough for Moses, it should be good enough for your ass!"

Grandma put the food in her mouth signaling the end of the discussion. Mom looked down at the table and shook her head.

"Shit," she muttered under her breath.

"Ooh, Mommy said a bad word," Tracie said in her singsong tone.

We ate politely. A short time later the waitress brought our check. I sneaked a look at it. Sixteen dollars. I watched as my mother opened her purse, took out two twenties, and slipped them under the check.

"Okay, let's go," she said.

"How much was it?" Grandma asked.

"Never mind. Let's go."

Grandma picked up the check and looked at it. She looked at the two twenties and then at the check again as if to make certain that she had read it correctly.

"Gal, what you doing?" she finally asked.

"I left a tip. Let's go."

Grandma reached for one of the twenties.

"This is too much money to be throwing away," she barked. The other diners were looking our way again.

"Leave it where it is!" my mother snapped, jolting us all to attention. "I'm not throwing it away."

There was a silence. It was a tense silence. Then again, I feel that all silences are tense. I hate dead air. She finally broke the impasse.

Staring into Grandma's eyes, she said, "Maybe the next black family this waitress serves will be treated a little better because this black family left her some money. Let's go. Please."

My mother. Never in moderation.

This gesture struck me, because here was my mother in all of her—I don't know, is "regality" the right word?—showing that she was better than that waitress. That she had more class. That it was actually possible to buy respect, for twenty-four bucks.

Earlier, I wrote that my mother wanted white children, that she wanted to be white. Actually, that's a cheap shot because it's not accurate. What my mother wanted was respect. The respect that white people seem to give each other based upon their common heritage. You see, black people have to "earn" the respect of white people, whereas white people grant it to each other based upon their pigment.

The funny thing is that I'm sure that that waitress had no

idea what that gesture was all about. She probably thought it was a mistake. Two twenties stuck together. Our tough luck, her good fortune.

My mother's gesture is one that impacts both me and Tracie to this very day. Many servers of all races have a preconceived notion that black people don't tip. In many cases they're right. (Tip? Shit, you're getting paid!) Still I hate being painted with that broad brush. As a result of that common belief, many times people of color will receive inferior service from waiters and waitresses because the servers figure, "Why should I knock myself out when they aren't going to leave me a tip, anyway?"

So, what happens? The black customer gets his check and thinks, "I got shitty service. I'm not tipping." To which the server is then able to reply, "See? Told you they don't tip," thus making the whole thing a self-fulfilling prophecy.

I find myself acting as my mom did. I not only tip every time, I *overtip*. Even if I get bad service. In a way, I guess I feel a responsibility to break the stereotype. I'm tipping so that the next black customer gets better treatment. Kind of like paying the bridge toll for the car behind me.

One question, though. When did tipping become a right that servers were entitled to? Growing up, it was always my understanding that a tip was an extra reward to show a waiter or waitress gratitude for superior service. I always thought that the word "tips" was an acronym for the phrase "To Insure Proper Service." If this is indeed the case, why is it now an entitlement? Moreover, why are there tip jars in places where you aren't even getting any kind of special service? Why is there a jar for tips next to the counter at Starbucks? I stood in line. I placed an order. The clerk handed me my order. I paid the menu price plus tax for said order. Why am I now expected to compensate you for handing me my latte?

I know what you're thinking, and you're right. I put money in the jar just so that the bohemian at the register won't think, "See? Black people don't tip." It's a vicious cycle.

The restaurant issue is a perfect example of how race wears on our society. If a white customer goes to a restaurant and gets bad service, more likely than not he thinks, "Gee, I got bad service." If a black customer goes to a restaurant and gets bad service, part of the evening is spent wondering, consciously or not, whether it was simply bad service or whether it was racism. White friends in the restaurant service industry have told me on several occasions about owners who instructed them to give blacks inferior service so that they wouldn't return.

One of the most egregious cases I've heard of involves a popular restaurant in the San Leandro/Hayward area that my mother took us to a few times when we were kids. Former employees have told me that it was a common practice in the 1960s and 1970s for the restaurant staff, at the direction of the management, to oversalt the food of black patrons to discourage their continued patronage. I remember thinking then that the food was kind of salty, but the place was packed. I figured that it must have been my pedestrian palate so I never said a word; nor did my mother. The only blacks in the place were not going to tell a building full of whites that the emperor had no clothes. And that he was too salty.

I'm not sure that Grandma agreed with my mother's reasoning that day at brunch, but she loved her and she indulged her, as we all did. Without saying another word, Grandma took her hands off of the money and we got up and left the restaurant.

After brunch, we went to the mall to shop . . . for housewares. Every kid's dream afternoon. A few years later (all right, a few hours but it *felt* like a few years) we were back in our apartment where I was finally taking off my itchy sport jacket when I was interrupted by a knocking at the front door. Actually, "knocking" isn't the right word. It was more like a *banging* or a *pounding*.

I went downstairs and opened the door to find a little blond girl, about my age; an older woman, apparently her mother; and a white mob, standing there. I'm talking about fifteen or twenty people all piled up on our little front porch and squeezed up against the green picket fence that surrounded the patio adjacent to the front door.

There was a little raggedy boy, about seven years old; a woman with her head tied up with a train engineer's bandana, a cigarette dripping from her lips; a teenage boy wearing a Confederate-flag tank top. I felt like Nostradamus looking at a *Jerry Springer* premonition.

The woman spoke to the little raggedy boy.

"Is this him?" she asked, pointing at me.

He nodded his head.

"Yeah, that's him."

Suddenly, she was inches from my face, her words spewing at me like so much bile.

"You keep your damned hands off of our cat!"

What cat? What is she talking about?

My mother appeared at the door behind me. She had been taking off her makeup and still had traces of face cream on her cheeks.

"Is there a problem?" she asked, putting her hand gently on my shoulder.

The woman backed away from my face a few inches, taking Mom in. My mother was a slight woman. She was demure and almost dainty, but she had a presence much larger than her actual physicality.

"Are you this boy's mother?" the woman said.

My mother's demeanor changed.

"First of all, don't you call my son a damned 'boy.'"

She could be black when she wanted to.

"I am this young man's mother," she continued. "What is the problem?"

The little blond girl spoke up.

"He threw my kitty in the pool!"

"No I didn't," I protested. "I didn't."

"Yeah he did. I saw him," the raggedy boy said, with a self-satisfied smirk on his face.

"The cat was missing," the woman said, with venomous animation, "and when we found her she was soaking wet and half-drowned."

She jabbed her finger in my direction. For a woman, it was a thick, meaty finger. It reminded me of a sausage link.

"The kids said that the black boy . . ."

My mother's stern glare forced her to rethink her choice of words.

"I mean, the black 'kid,' who lives here, threw her in the swimming pool."

"My son did not touch your cat," Mom said. She was calm. Reasoned. *I'm not going to lose control.*

"He's allergic to cats."

Now the raggedy boy was pointing at me.

"Yeah, he did. I saw him."

"When?" my mother asked. "When did you see my son throw a cat or anything else in that swimming pool?"

The answer was quick.

"Today. A couple hours ago."

My mother maintained her cool.

"You're clearly mistaken. He's been with me all day. We

went to mass, then we went to brunch, and then we went shopping. We just got home."

The little girl spoke up again.

"Mommy, what's 'brunch'?"

It felt good knowing that my mom had my back like that. There were so many people out there accusing me, I thought for a minute, "Shit, maybe I did try to drown the damned cat."

The woman was adamant.

"We have witnesses," she said, every word enunciated with clipped precision.

"Well," Mom said, "they're either mistaken, or they're lying."

"Well, you are the only colored people around here and . . ."

There went Mom's cool.

"And *you* had better get the hell off of my doorstep."

"And who's gonna make me?"

Suddenly there was a splash. Then steam. The woman got all red-faced. Steam rose from the little boy's head. The teenage boy started crying. What the hell just happened?

I looked at my mom and a sly smile crept across her lips. I noticed that she was looking over my shoulder at the patio. There, on the other side of the green picket fence, stood Grandma, holding a steaming pot. She had been boiling water to cook some greens but found a better use for it.

There was outrage, pandemonium, cussing. The woman went ballistic.

"You niggers!" she screamed. "You fucking niggers!"

Mom had my back and Grandma had hers.

"Come on inside, son," she said gently.

We went inside and closed the door, and then she hugged me really tight. When I was a kid, my mother's arms were like a blanket to me. A blanket keeping me warm when the world was so cold. A blanket that smelled like Jean Naté products.

This was different, though. She was shaking. For the first time, I was holding her.

"It's okay, Mommy," I tried to comfort. "They're gone. It's okay. They're gone."

"Doggone right they gone," said a disembodied voice.

Grandma stood in the doorway looking strangely satisfied. She'd been vindicated. She wasn't paranoid. That day, for the first time in my life, I learned the difference between paranoia and legitimate concern. Who knows? We might have been blamed for poisoned candy on Halloween. The world just got a lot scarier.

"You know," she said, "it's a good thing you was with us today or they could have said you did any kind of mess."

I think that this was a defining moment for Grandma, being able to strike back like that. Don't get me wrong. My grandmother has never been anybody's doormat, but pouring hot water on irate white people? You don't do that in Birmingham.

"Carolyn," Grandma bellowed, "what's wrong with you?"

"I'm sorry," she said through streams of tears. "I'm so sorry. I never should have moved us here."

"Sorry, shit!" Grandma shouted. "We got just as much right to be here as they got."

"But it's so hard on the kids, Suer. So hard on Brian."

It was hard for me to see her like this. Unsure. Vulnerable. Human.

"I'm okay, Mom," I said. "Honest."

My train of thought was broken by another knock at the front door. Jesus, how hot was that water? Could the cops have gotten here that fast? What was I thinking? There were black people involved. Of course the cops could be there "that fast."

Grandma ran off to the kitchen to get some more hot water.

My mother sat down on her plastic couch to compose herself. I headed for the door. Mom stopped me.

"Wait," she said through black trails of mascara.

"It's okay, Mom. I'm the man of the house, remember?"

She gave me a weary smile. Maybe I really *was* the man of the house.

I went to the door and opened it, slowly at first, just a crack in case I had to shut it fast. Hurry up with the hot water, Grandma.

I peered through the crack in the door to see Mr. Wentworth, the apartment manager, standing on the porch. Wentworth was a fiftyish guy who always wore a sky blue jumpsuit that was about two sizes too small for his chubby ass. Wentworth was one of those "nice" racists. Always kind and convivial in your face. Jovial and congenial with an overcompensated friendliness that came across as insincere even in the mind of an eight-year-old.

"Hey there young fella!" he said in his smarmy way.

"Hi, Mr. Wentworth."

"I've got something to give your mama. I came by earlier and knocked but nobody answered."

"We were at brunch."

"Brunch? What's that?"

Where did my mother come up with this stuff?

"Kind of like 'leakfast,'" I explained. It was as good an explanation as any. "I'll take it."

He handed me a white legal envelope with my mother's name typed on it. I got a queasy feeling in my stomach. What was it about typewriters? The *clickity clack* of the keys has always made me uneasy. It brought back memories of all of the places I hated most as a kid: doctors' and principals' offices.

"Now you make sure she gets that, son," he said, his bullshit smile plastered across his face.

"Yeah," I said, closing the door just as Grandma came running in with another steaming pot. "Mr. Wentworth, Grandma."

She stamped her foot. "Shit!"

I walked over to the couch where my mother appeared to be in better shape now. Though her eyes were still red and puffy, I could feel her struggling to regain the self-discipline she'd spent a lifetime developing. She straightened her body and sat rigidly upright. She sniffled softly and ran the knuckle of her right index finger under her nose. Control. Always under control.

"Mr. Wentworth, Mom. He said to give you this."

She took the envelope and opened it. She then took out a white sheet of legal-size paper and stared at it for a long time.

"What is it, Mom? What's wrong?"

Dead air again. I didn't know how long it lasted, only that, once again, it was too long. Finally she looked up from the paper.

"We're being evicted."

CHAPTER 13

Daddy Knows the Great Unknown

I t was 1999. Grandma had just called. She wanted to know if I would go to the cemetery with her and the girls on Sunday. Sunday. Twenty years. She had been gone for *twenty years*. She was twenty when she had me. That meant I was now her age. That meant that this year, I'd outlive her.

My mother died three months before my fifteenth birthday. Sarchoidosis. It's a lung disease that afflicts primarily black women. Ironic, isn't it? As hard as she had tried to run away from her heritage, in the end, she couldn't.

The question that the guys had asked me on my birthday popped into my head. The question I had avoided answering. The thing I try never to think about. When did I first feel like a grown-up? I know the exact moment that my childhood ended. I was fourteen and Mom had been dead for about ten minutes. Grandma and I were standing in the hospital waiting room. She was crying. In my fourteen years on this earth, I had never seen Grandma cry. Surprisingly, I wasn't crying. I was numb. I was in shock. Mom had been in the hospital for three weeks and was supposed to be going home the following day. Suddenly, she went into cardiac arrest, then heart failure. Then she died . . . at age thirty-five.

The doctor came out and offered me and Grandma his condolences. Grandma didn't hear him. She just kept saying over and over, "What we gon' do, Brian? What we gon' do?"

I was patting her on the back, trying to offer her some comfort when the doctor said, "I'd like to perform an autopsy."

Grandma looked up, her face wet with tears. It was almost more than I could bear.

"I'll need your permission before we can proceed," he continued.

There was silence as he stood looking at Grandma. Grandma turned and looked at me. The look was like a transference, like one of those bad body-switching movies from the '80s. I was suddenly the adult and she was the distraught child.

"You tell him what you want to do," she said.

It was left to me, fourteen-year-old me, to decide whether or not I'd allow these butchers to carve up my mother's body. After telling the doctor that I wouldn't allow her to be violated in that manner, I blocked the moment out. I pushed it down with all of the other sewage of my life. I drowned it in drink and in work and in hubris. It worked, until now. Until I was thirty-five; her age. The sewage had finally backed up.

I'd achieved everything she wanted me to and more. I lived in the nicest neighborhood in town, a neighborhood in which she would have been stopped just for walking through. I had a great family. I worked in television and radio. I worked on stage as the opening act for some of the biggest stars in show business. I even had an audience with the president of the United States. I was middle class. Hell, I was upper middle class.

I had spent the first fifteen years of my life trying to please my mother, and the last twenty trying to *be* my mother. Was that what was wrong?

Was it that stuff way back at the hobby shop with my son that ripped the scabs off of old wounds that had never healed, could that have been it? Or was it that I just didn't know who I was?

It could have been some of those things. It could have been all of those things. Those four hurtful words rang in my head again. I guess that in a way, they've always been there.

"He's still a nigger."

The words were loud in the empty house, my family out for the evening. It was just as well. I didn't want anybody around at that moment.

I hung up the phone and went into the kitchen. I opened the cupboard and took out my silver martini shaker and a martini glass. I filled the shaker with crushed ice and I poured in Russian vodka and silently counted to myself as I watched the stream of clear liquid saturate the ice. *One thousand one, one thousand two, one thousand three, one thousand four, one thousand five, one thousand six.*

I sat the bottle on the counter. What the hell? I picked the bottle up again. *One thousand seven, one thousand eight, one thousand nine.*

I poured in vermouth. Just a drop. I like my martinis dry. Like James Bond. That's not black, is it?

I shook it up, poured the elixir into the martini glass, and dropped in a lemon peel. I grabbed the drink and went into the living room where I kept my big oak humidor. I took out a Cohiba Churchill. Cuban. I'd snuck it into the country from Mexico after my last vacation. (If customs should ask you, I never wrote this part.) I snipped the end of the cigar with my shiny V cutter and I lit it.

I took the drink and the cigar and went out into the garage. I closed all of the doors. I put the top down on my sportscar and I climbed in. I started the motor. I put in a CD of my favorite album from high school—Rick Springfield's *Success*

Hasn't Spoiled Me Yet. (Definitely *not* black.) I listened to the melancholic song he sings about losing his father suddenly. I felt his longing as he ponders the hereafter and takes comfort in the fact that his daddy now knows the great unknown. The great unknown. Mom knows it, too. Soon, so would I.

I downed the martini and threw the empty glass on the passenger seat. I took a drag from the cigar. The smoke was smooth. Cool.

I gently placed the cigar in the ashtray, leaned back, closed my eyes, listened to the motor idle, and I breathed. It was Tuesday. I was born on a Tuesday, too.

PART 2

"Where should we talk about race? Everywhere. It's not an African-American issue or an Asian issue. It is an American issue."

—Senator John Edwards,
July 28, 2004

CHAPTER 14

Fighting Back

"Our city is not a 'white spot' by accident. Individual realtors through 'gentlemen's agreements' have been 'selective' in determining renters and buyers."

> —San Leandro City Councilman Joseph Gancos, March 1969

y mother looked weary as she trudged up the stairs, her eyes glued to the eviction notice she had just received. I heard her go into her room and close the door. I went into the kitchen and picked up the extension. Mom's voice.

"I don't understand this."

"Well, what's there to understand?" came the terse and condescending reply.

It was Mrs. Wentworth, the landlady. Actually, "landbitch" would've been more accurate.

"You have fifteen days to vacate the premises," she snapped at my mother.

"But why? For what reason?"

"We're no longer renting to families your size. You'll have to leave."

"You can't do this."

"Listen, you nigger, don't tell me what I can and can't do in my own building."

Did she really say that? To my mother? This hurt me. This hurt even more than the redheaded kid on the kickball diamond. She called my mother that name. *My mother!*

I could feel the familiar sting of the tears welling up in my eyes. Funny, after everything that had happened that day—the angry mob, the hot water, the notice to vacate—you'd think that the tears would have already come by now. Maybe I was tougher than I thought.

"We'll see," my mother finally said. Her tone was strange. It was as if the words stuck in her throat and she was fighting to release them. Like the word "nigger" was a blow to her gut that expelled all of the air from her body, making it impossible to emit sound, impossible to vocalize the pain, the hurt, the astonishment, and the indignity. Liberal Northern California.

"We'll see," she said again.

A few minutes later, my mother came bounding down the stairs. She seemed reinvigorated. Alive. Determined. There was that joker again.

"I'm going to sue the bastards."

CHAPTER 15

The City's Conscience

"I have been quite outspoken on the issue of open housing in our community. A member of my congregation had a home for rent and asked for my assistance in finding a suitable tenant. He said that race was not a problem. Unfortunately, race was a problem for many in my congregation. Upon showing the home in question to negro families, half the members left my church. I did talk to them and the response by and large was, 'We like the negroes. We really do. We have many negro friends and we're not opposed to equal rights per se. We just don't feel that you have any business talking about it from the pulpit. You should stick solely to the gospels.' Now, they would never admit that they were basically prejudiced, and who am I to judge and to say that that is the reason for their anger and their hostility, but it does appear to me that much of their resistance really is reflecting a deep-seated prejudice."

—Rev. Dorel Londagin, San Leandro pastor of Christ
Presbyterian Church in testimony before the U.S. Commission
on Civil Rights hearings, May 6, 1967

Dorel Londagin was a very interesting guy in that he never stopped fighting for civil rights. He was, for lack of a better phrase, San Leandro's conscience. Born in Oklahoma, Rev. Londagin had a deep sense of social justice. As a young minister in the 1950s, he caused a major stir among his Oklahoman congregation when he refused to sit in the dining room of a restaurant after a black woman, who was part of a church outing he was leading, was refused service. When the woman was told that she could take her meal in the kitchen where blacks were served, Londagin went and ate with her.

In 1952, he was named the founding pastor of Christ Presbyterian Church, a half block up the street from our apartment complex. His congregation grew and the church thrived until the good reverend began challenging the de facto segregation in the community.

In the mid 1960s, Londagin invited the mostly black congregation of a Presbyterian church from the nearby city of Emeryville to a picnic with his flock. The event was to be held in Washington Manor Park (the park I was looking for on my first venture outside of our apartment). People called the minister's home and threatened to kill him and his family if he "brought those niggers into this town."

Rev. Londagin was a family man with a wife and young children. Mrs. Londagin was terrified for their safety, but understood the conviction of her husband's principles and urged him to go ahead and hold the event. The picnic took place without incident, though, as expected, the participation by Londagin's church members was less than overwhelming.

Things hit crisis mode during the attempt to rent a congregant's home, referred to in the testimony recounted above. Despite the opposition from his church members, the minister persisted in trying to get a black family into the neighborhood. According to Londagin's daughter, Beth Wilcoxin, he came close.

"A young black couple was all set to sign a rental contract for the property," she said. "They were sitting in my parents' living room finalizing the agreement, when suddenly the woman burst into tears and said that she couldn't do it. She said that she knew about the hostility of the people in town and feared what they would do to them."

With that, Rev. Londagin abandoned his efforts to rent that particular home. He didn't, however, abandon his quest to integrate the community. A couple of years after he testified before the commission, half of the remaining members of his congregation deserted when Rev. Londagin partnered with Temple Beth Shalom and supported the construction of a senior citizens' housing facility that would be open to black people. The building went up and is an integrated senior-living home to this day, but it devastated the minister's church.

With his congregation too small to support a full-time pastor, Rev. Londagin switched careers and decided to fight for equal rights another way. He became a San Leandro Realtor.

CHAPTER 16

Waking Up Is Hard to Do

I was lying on a hospital gurney. A clear plastic oxygen mask covered my nose and mouth. My right leg was tethered to the gurney. Well, it wasn't actually a tether; it was more like a belt. A leather belt with a buckle. That was so I couldn't escape. It was a leather belt with a buckle so that I couldn't escape.

I don't know how many times in my life I've struggled with the belt around my waist thinking, "I have to go to the bathroom but I can't figure out how you operate this goddamned thing!"

If they really wanted to keep me there, why didn't they tether my hands together or something? I suppose that would have been too logical.

I lay there pondering various Houdini scenarios as two cops walked in. The first one spoke to me.

"Do you know where you are?"

His voice had a hint of Boston. Isn't that the city where that husband shot his pregnant wife in the head and blamed a black carjacker? The cops spent days rousting every male over the age of twelve and darker than a brown paper bag until the guilty husband jumped off a bridge. I can't get away from it, can I?

"Do you know where you are?" he asked me again.

Yeah, I knew where I was. A lot better off than I had been a couple of hours before. I had awakened in the garage to the firm grip of a hand on my shoulder. Through bleary eyes, I followed the hand up the sleeve to the mug of a freckle-faced police officer.

Do you mean to tell me, that after everything I've been through, that St. Peter is a white motherfucking cop?? This is some bullshit.

It turned out that one of the neighbors had heard music blaring in the garage and called the police because she thought that something might be amiss. That's what white people do. They notice when things are *"amiss."* Since there was no telling how long I'd been breathing in fumes, I was rushed by ambulance to the hospital.

"Do you know where you are?" Boston repeated.

"I'm in Highland Hospital in Oakland."

Highland is the county hospital. It's where they send the uninsured, the drive-by-shooting victims, and the crazies. Mom had worked there as a secretary in the '70s. In the psych ward as I recall. I had come full circle.

"So," Boston said, "what was going on out there?"

"I guess I fell asleep."

"Why were you trying to hurt yourself?"

"Is that what you think? No. No. I was just having a cigar and a martini when I noticed that my car was in the driveway. I put it in the garage, started listening to music, and I guess I fell asleep. With the motor running," I added, almost as an afterthought.

He looked at me with skepticism in his eyes.

"What were all the pictures?"

I'd forgotten that I'd brought pictures out there with me. Grandma, my kids, and Mom.

"My sister wanted me to get some copies made. I haven't gotten around to it yet."

"Why were you trying to hurt yourself," he said again with a sigh. He'd heard these bullshit denials a million times.

I exploded.

"I wasn't! I was listening to Rick Springfield for God's sake."

I saw some hope. I could tell that he was fighting a smile.

"Look," I babbled, "I was just having a cigar and a martini in my closed garage, listening to music with pictures when I fell asleep with the motor running. Like that's never happened to you!"

Yeah, I know. It even sounded crazy to me when I said it.

He nodded his head sympathetically.

"All right, I'll tell you what we're gonna do, here. We're gonna hold you on a 5150. That means you're a danger to yourself or others. We can keep you for up to seventy-two hours for observation."

He put his hand on my shoulder and looked into my eyes.

"It'll be okay. You get some rest."

I cast my eyes downward, looking at the strap on my leg. How in the world had it come to this?

"Yeah," I whispered.

He headed for the door, with the other officer following behind him. After the first cop walked out, the second one, who up to this point hadn't said a word, turned and looked at me. Wait. I think I know this guy.

I studied him through the muddled haze that fogged my brain. His hair was not as blond and the mirrored sunglasses were gone. No. It couldn't be. Could it? I pictured him thrusting my baseball bat in my mother's face.

"He was using this as a weapon. That's very serious."

Could he have transferred to Oakland? Or was my mind playing tricks on me? Did that cop become every cop in my eyes?

Suddenly he was walking toward me. Was it the same guy, and did he recognize me, too?

As he approached, he put his hands in his pocket and took out a pad and pen.

"Mr. Copeland?" he said obsequiously, sticking the writing implements in my face. "My wife is a really big fan. Would you mind?"

I've been asked for autographs in some weird places around the Bay Area, from dentist chairs to rosaries for the dead to men's room urinals, but this was a first.

"Sure," I said, taking the paper and pen. "What's her name?"

"Phyllis."

"To Phyllis" I scratched on the pad, stopping suddenly when I had an epiphany.

This is why they didn't tether my hands together!

Celebrity is a strange thing. I'm only a regional celebrity and here I had gone from being hassled by the police simply for existing as a black child, to signing autographs for their wives after being involuntarily committed.

CHAPTER 17

A Great Big Can of Worms

"Attitudes of some Realtors are reflected in these actual quotes:

'Our prices are high enough to keep them out . . .'

'We can control it (entry of minorities into the city) with our prices.'

'Thank god our prices are too high for them . . . they can't raise a dime.'

'I don't want to do business with niggers . . .'

'I have told the neighbors they don't have to worry . . .'

'Nobody would tell you anything on the phone, they have to see what color you are.'

'If you write 'white' on the card, the Realtors will call you . . .' "

—San Leandro Fair Housing Committee Report—January 24, 1972

The case of *Carolyn Copeland v. Ronald Starr* (the owner of the apartment complex), *and Harold and Connie Wentworth* (the apartment managers) *et al* was filed in Alameda County Superior Court in the spring of 1973. My mother sued for housing discrimination and intentional infliction of emotional distress.

This meant that if she won, we'd get to stay in San Leandro longer! Oh goody. First prize—a week in San Leandro. Second prize—two weeks in San Leandro.

The judge had put a hold on the eviction so that it could not go forward until after the matter came to trial. It would take two years for the case to get to trial. Two years during which a lot of really strange things happened.

A sewer pipe burst under our apartment unit and it reeked like garbage for days. Nobody else's, just ours. Four times the doorknob to our front door was bashed in with a crowbar. The police said that they were burglary attempts. Then there were the phone calls. Sometimes there would just be hang-ups. Other times someone would whisper the word "nigger."

My mother began missing things from her bedroom, primarily papers and documents pertaining to her case. Then one day, I was home alone, sick in bed with the flu, when there was a noise at the front door.

The noise made me bolt straight up in bed. Was it another burglary attempt? I slowly slipped from under my covers, grabbed my junior Louisville Slugger and crept down the stairs. I didn't know what I was gonna do if there was somebody in there. I guess, hit them with the label side up. I wasn't cracking my birthday bat.

Not that it mattered, anyway. I may have owned the bat but I was no good at using it. The way I played, even if I confronted a prowler, I wouldn't have been able to connect with his body in three swings.

I got to the bottom of the staircase where I was greeted with a startled, "Hey there young fella!"

Mr. Wentworth. What was he doing in here?

"I'm looking for your mama."

I clutched the bat tightly, keeping it conspicuously in striking position.

"She's at work, like she usually is at ten-thirty on a Thursday morning."

"Oh. Well, she wanted me to fix some things around here. I must have written it down wrong on my calendar. I'll be back later."

Wentworth looked me in the eyes, his mouth wide with a fidgety smile.

"Wait a minute," I thought. "This is bullshit! My mother hires outside repair people to fix things. She doesn't trust any of these losers."

I moved toward him, the bat still resting on my shoulder, my grip on its base firm. As I moved closer, he retreated. The grin on his face tightened. He looked like his face was contorted with rigor mortis, the smile was so tight; an eerie death grin.

I watched as Wentworth let himself out and locked the door with his pass key.

CHAPTER 18

Mixed Messages

My childhood was a confusing barrage of mixed messages. On the one hand, Mom would say, "Be proud that you're black, because black is beautiful." Then, when we acted up, she and Grandma would say, "Act your age, not your color," as if immaturity, rambunctiousness and negative behavior were "black" things. Did that make good behavior a "white" trait? If that was the case, then why was so much of the bad behavior directed toward me coming from white people?

The discrepancy was glaring to me. Every time I heard the word "black" it was in a negative context. A litany of images overloaded my senses with the less-than-subtle implication that there was something negative associated with things black.

In school, we learned that the day the stock market crashed in 1929 was "Black Tuesday." On the news, I heard difficult times, such as the Watergate affair and the war in Vietnam, described as "Black days in our nation's history." Funeral processions I'd see on the street were led by bodies carried in black hearses. Mourners dressed in black. "Black clouds coming in" meant unpleasant weather ahead. Other than the occasional black comedian like Bill Cosby or Flip Wilson, the blacks that I saw on television were being led away in handcuffs. Murderous radicals, who instilled fear in me simply by the way that their names were ominously intoned by television newscasters, shared my pigment. The Black Panthers, the Black Muslims, and Cinque, the leader of the Symbionese Liberation Army, which had kidnapped newspaper heiress Patty Hearst from her home in nearby Berkeley. All inspiring dread, panic, and trepidation, all looking like me.

The mobs that gathered at the food distribution stations the SLA had demanded Randolph Hearst establish as his daughter's ransom, the mob that rioted and behaved like a pack of wild animals over the free vittles, looked like me. Sylvester looked like me. Even in old cowboy movies I'd see on the *Late Late Late Show* (I'm dating myself with *that* reference), the bad guys wore black hats.

On the other hand, the good guys wore white hats. Commercials touted detergents that made "whites whiter." The "whiter," the better. The communion host at mass, the actual body of Jesus Christ himself, was white. I'd hear women speak of wanting to have a white wedding. The seat of American power was the White House.

To try and make sense of it all, I did what my mother always told me to do when I was in search of information. I looked it up. Even the thesaurus reinforced the perception. It defined "white" as *innocent, pure, unsullied, stainless, unblemished, spotless, immaculate, virginal, virtuous, undefiled,* and *chaste.* It defined "Caucasians" as *fair-skinned.* The skin of white people denotes "fairness"! White was clean. White was pure and virginal. Like the driven snow. Did this mean that I wasn't these things?

The thesaurus defined "black" as *somber, gloomy, menacing, lowering, threatening, malignant, deadly, sinister, dismal, hateful, disastrous, bad, foul, wicked, evil, diabolical, hellish, atrocious, awful, malicious, abominable, vicious, villainous, vile, disgraceful, unscrupulous, unconscionable, unprincipled, insidious, nefarious, dastardly, treacherous, unspeakable, shameful, criminal, felonious, angry, wrathful, furious, frowning, bad-tempered, sulky, resentful,* and *glowering.*

At least "black" got more thesaurus space.

It was a gray morning as we walked to school. It was just the three of us on the one-mile trek. Tracie, Delisa, and me. I was in charge, responsible for the girls' well-being. If anything happened to them, anything at all, it would be my fault. More accurately, it would be my ass. I held Delisa by the wrist, like Grandma did. She was a little first grader and she had a tendency to straggle and wander off. Not on my watch.

"You're walking too fast," Delisa complained.

"No, I'm not. We can't be late. We *won't* be late. We're going to be on time."

"I can't keep up and you're squishing my arm."

"Yeah, Brian," Tracie said. "Slow down. I'm sweating."

"Sweat then!" I said.

"Why don'cha let the li'l gals catch they breath?" the voice said. The drawl was Southern and as thick as heavy fog.

I ignored it and kept walking.

"Ah say, why don'cha slow up so the li'l gals can catch they breath?"

I saw the old man standing across the street. He appeared to be ancient. He had a large round face. Wisps of silky gray ornamented his mostly bald pate. Thick, black glasses with even thicker lenses rested on the bridge of his nose, which had prominent veins and capillaries treading through it, reminiscent of a AAA road map. A medium-sized beach ball protruded from his midsection. He was a large man. His frame was imposing. I could tell that in his youth, he was powerful; formidable, even.

Delisa stopped dead in her tracks. I was now dragging her across the sidewalk; her black patent-leather shoes scraped loudly across the concrete.

"Come on," I yelled. I wasn't talking to strangers, especially not strangers with a Southern drawl.

"Y'all can't speak?" he shouted.

"Hi," Tracie said, waving.

He pulled a hand from the pocket of the filthy denim coveralls that he wore over a crisp white shirt. Black dirt and a clean white shirt. Dichotomy. More mixed messages.

"Hey, there," he said. The word "there" came out as *theah*. His words had a barking quality. Short. Staccato.

I snatched Tracie's hand down.

"Come on!" I hurried my pace.

"I just waved," she said.

"Don't!" It was me who barked now.

"But," she pleaded, "Mommy always says to be polite. She always says to be 'ladies and gentlemen.'"

"Not now! Not to him!"

I was dragging them both now. Delisa with my left hand, Tracie with my right, struggling as I tried to hold on to both their wrists and my lunch bag at the same time. We were getting out of there.

I knew this guy. I knew *all* about him. I had just watched a show about Martin Luther King Jr. with Grandma the previous night. The anniversary of his murder was coming up and there were stories about him everywhere. I didn't know much about Martin Luther King Jr. I knew that I was almost four when he was killed. I was watching TV with my mom when the news bulletin broke in. I remember watching her cry and I remember that for what seemed like an eternity, there was nothing on television but sadness and tears, rage and rioting, punctuated by brief periods of somber remembrance and reflection. The show that I watched with Grandma had shown me more. Horrifyingly more.

I watched the grainy footage of men with clubs beating black people. I saw the fury in their eyes as they threw rocks and bricks at children; children just like me who were only marching, singing, and clapping. I heard the horde's gleeful laughter as they let loose snarling dogs to bite and tear at the flesh of people peacefully sitting in the streets and praying. I saw the policemen and the firemen assist with the carnage, the force of the water from their hoses washing the blacks down the street like so much dirt swept from a suburban driveway into the drainage gutter and down the sewer. I watched the interviews where the members of the mob justified their brutality. Rationalizations peppered with the phrases, "nigger" this and "nigger" that. Justifications uttered with a drawl. A drawl where the word "there" was pronounced *theah*.

I had never set foot in the South in my life. I had never before set eyes on this man shouting at us from across the street. I didn't know his name, his occupation, or his origins. But I felt that I knew him. I had just watched an evening of televised nightmares starring men just like him.

"Don't look at him," I instructed the girls as I rushed them down the street out of the man's line of sight. "Keep your eyes straight ahead and don't look at him!"

"Bye, y'all," the voice yelled after us.

It was a few days later, as I walked home from school. It was Friday. Good Friday, the last day before Easter break. A whole week without school. This time, I was alone. My sisters had a Girl Scout function and would get a ride home from Grandma later. As I meandered down my street, I daydreamed about all of the delicious freedom that lay ahead.

I pictured Easter baskets overflowing with sugary goodies. Mom still thought that I believed there was an Easter Bunny who would creep into our apartment on Holy Saturday night and leave me cavity-inducing treats. I had figured this scam out ages ago, but I would do what it took to reap the rewards. If ignorance was bliss—made real in the form of chocolate rabbits and jelly beans—I would play along. I'd even go so far as to not question what a big rabbit with colored eggs had to do with the resurrection of Jesus Christ. What in the world is the connection between the death of our Savior and an Easter-egg hunt?

What happened when the women found Christ's tomb empty?

Woman #1: The body of the Lord is missing.

Woman #2: Maybe we should look under the couch.

I'm Catholic, so I don't ask questions. I learned that with Christmas. A fat man in a red suit who spends his days at the mall promising kids toys if they'll sit on his lap. That's not religious. That's creepy. Even more so when Grandma told us, as we struggled in our excitement to fall asleep on Christmas Eve, that if we were awake when Santa Claus came, he'd put ashes in our eyes. Ashes! You get gifts or you're blinded. There is the true spirit of Christmas. God bless us, every one.

I had been saving my allowance and I had two dollars in my pocket. Enough for ten comic books. I couldn't wait to go to 7-Eleven for my fix. It was the thing I most looked forward to in the world. There was something exciting, yet at the same time soothing, about the squeaky sound of the metal magazine racks as I slowly spun them, mesmerized by the flashes of bright color and the smell of comic book paper. Before me was another world I could escape to. A world where good always triumphed over evil. A world where nothing was impossible. I thought of how I would spend the next week soaring over the skies of Metropolis with Superman, running through the streets of Central City with the Flash and stealthily lurking over the rooftops of Gotham City with Batman.

I was so deep in my fantasies that I didn't even hear them behind me. I just felt the breeze of the rock as it whizzed past my left ear. I turned around just as the next stone made contact with my right shoulder. It was a small stone and it startled me more than hurt me. The third stone was bigger and caught me on the forehead. I felt a cold numbness in my nasal cavity. A constellation of stars appeared, blinding me.

As I rubbed the confusion from my eyes, I saw them. There were three white boys. Two appeared bigger than me. The third was a little runt with a black knit Oakland Raiders beanie covering his head.

As far as I could tell, I'd never seen the boys before. Another rock creased my scalp. I felt that fear-based adrenaline rush. My legs took off. I didn't command them to, they just ran. I thought of the Flash, running faster than the speed of sound, moving so quickly he could run across bodies of water because his feet don't have time to sink, skimming the liquid like a stone skipping across a pond on a summer afternoon. I thought how badly I needed his super speed as the footsteps behind me got louder. They were faster, closer, and mingled with gleeful delight and laughter.

Another rock hit me square between the shoulder blades. It stung like hell. My feet didn't stop as I heard theirs getting closer still. The next thing I knew, my back was against the garage of one of the houses that lined the block. I didn't know how I got there, but it was a deadly mistake. A dumb tactical error. Now I was cornered. The boys stood in front of me in a semicircle and I had no place to run. Stupid. Why did I do this? Batman would never have let himself get trapped like this.

I was outnumbered so fighting them was out of the question. Even if it were one against one, unless I squared off against the runt of the litter, it wouldn't be a fair fight. I wouldn't have a prayer. The other two were husky, older. So much so that I was half surprised they didn't hop in a car and drive after me.

I covered my face with my arms as more stones were hurled my way. I felt like the harlot in an Old Testament Bible story, the angry mob stoning her for her illicit transgressions. I was the condemned in a twisted firing squad. I didn't even know what my crime was. They could have at least offered me a blindfold and a cigarette. Another rock hit me in the forearm. Then another. And another. Tears welled up in my eyes, but I wouldn't let them fall. They would never see me cry. They could beat me, bruise me, stone me, kill me if they had to, but they would not make me cry.

The onslaught continued unabated. Where were they getting all of these rocks? Had they chased me with rock-filled pockets? Then how did they move so fast? I guess I'm not the Flash after all.

I covered my eyes with my hands.

"Leave him be!" I heard the voice say.

Another rock hit me in the kneecap.

"Damn it, I said leave him be! Now!"

The voice was familiar. I'd heard it before. The bark. The drawl.

There was a startled reprieve. The rocks stopped coming. I slowly peeked through my fingers. The boys stood like statues, looking off to the side, their attention no longer on me.

"Get on 'way from here!" the drawl said, the word "here" sounding like *heah*.

I glanced in the direction that the boys were looking. The creepy old man stood there, angry. The veins in his neck popped out, the fire in his spectacled eyes magnified by the thickness of his coke-bottle lenses. He gripped a large metal pitchfork in his burly hands. A pitchfork! I had never even seen a pitchfork in real life. Just in that painting of the old farmer and his wife. American something or other. Just on the opening credits of *Green Acres*. There was nothing funny about the way the man was holding this one. It was a weapon. He was in attack position. I didn't know you could actually be in attack position with a pitchfork. Eddie Albert had the potential to be one bad-ass motherfucker.

"I said for y'all to get your asses on 'way from here," he commanded, shaking the implement as he inched toward my tormentors.

"NOW!" he shouted.

The small boy turned and ran. The other two hesitated for a moment and then followed their cowardly companion. I saw them disappear around the nearest street corner. I stung all over. I was bleeding from my forehead. A thin stream of crimson trickled down my right cheek. They were gone. Now the tears could come, and they did. I let out a few sniffles which soon gave way to sobs.

"Now, there ain't no need for all of that," the drawl said.

The sobs were heavier now. Louder. My chest heaved. Snot trickled down my nose and across my lips. I was a mess of tears, blood, and mucous. I had never realized how many fluids the body holds.

"Come on inside," the man said.

I stood in my place. Now it was my turn to be a statue.

"It's okay. Come on inside and let me clean some of that blood off of ya. You don't want to go home to your mama bleeding like that, do you? You'll scare the poor gal half to death."

I stood still. What do I do? I didn't know this man. Maybe it was a trick. He probably had a cellar where he buried little black boys like me. Or maybe he had some of those "black-people-eating dogs" from the Martin Luther King Jr. film. Maybe it was their feeding time and he was serving Purina Negro. I'd go inside and never be heard from again.

"I say come on, now!" he bellowed.

My body complied though my mind urged it to stay put. I trudged behind him, slowly, cautiously, as he walked up his driveway and then around the side of his garage into a side door.

"You wait right here," he said as he went into another door that apparently led into the house.

The smell in the garage hit me immediately: sawdust. The floor of the place was covered with it. An assortment of manual saws and wood-carving implements hung neatly arranged on the wall. There was a metal vise clamping some kind of wooden dowel. A small saw was frozen in the center of a rod it had been busily chewing along before being interrupted. A hand-held power saw sat nearby on a workbench.

On the other side of the garage were two shelves lined with handmade wooden knickknacks: a baby-doll bed, birdhouses of various sizes, a smoothly sanded train engine. Below the shelves was a beautiful cherrywood dining table. It had been stained a deep reddish brown. Next to the table was a large china cabinet. Mom just bought one for our apartment, but it was not nearly as nice as this one. I stood marveling at the workmanship as the man came back out carrying a towel and some bandages.

"I made that," he said, indicating the china cabinet.

"All by yourself?"

"Yep. Sure did. I made all of these things," he said, "things" coming out of his mouth as *thangs*.

He handed me the towel. It was cool and damp.

"Put that on your forehead. It'll stop the swelling."

My reluctance fading, I complied.

"What's your name, son?" he asked.

I hesitated for a moment. Mom always said not to give my name to strangers. I was not to give any personal information to people I didn't know. Not under any circumstances. Once, when I was home alone, I answered the phone and talked to a woman who said that she was an old classmate of Mom's from high school back in Akron. We chatted for an hour as she told me about what Mom was like as a teenager and how they used to hang out together and double date to the drive in movies and how scared Mom was of Godzilla. I answered her questions about how we were doing. I told her where we lived and where my mother worked. I even gave her Mom's work number so that she could call and surprise her. The woman said that they hadn't spoken in years. It had been longer than that, actually.

It turned out that the woman was a bill collector, gathering information on my mom's financial situation and personal data. I got my ass chewed out royally when the woman called Mom at her job. I didn't know. I was just seven at the time. I wasn't used to the idea that adults lied to kids and tricked them.

The man handed me some tissues to wipe my running nose. His move was sudden and it startled me. I jumped as he thrust the Kleenex in my direction.

"It's okay, young man. I'm not gone hurt ya. What's your name?"

"Brian," I answered softly, against my better instincts. "Just don't ask me where my mom works," I thought, "because I'm not telling."

He put his hand out to shake mine.

"I'm Josiah Wilkins. Nice to meet you, Brian."

I shook his hand. It was big, meaty, and rough. A worker's hand.

"Thank you for helping me, Mr. Wilkins."

I put the wet towel on a nearby workbench and moved toward the garage door. I was stopped by his hand on my shoulder.

"It's Josiah. Mr. Wilkins was my daddy and he's been dead a long time. You call me Josiah."

"My grandma says that I should always call grownups 'mister,' 'miss,' and 'missus.'"

He thought for a moment.

"Your Grandmama sounds like a right proper lady. Where is she from?"

Here we go. I turned into a mime again.

"Okay, then. I don't want you goin' against what your people are tellin' ya to do. I expect I can be Mr. Wilkins for *you*. *Only* for you. Just don't let it git around."

He winked at me and smiled. I felt a drop of warm blood drip down my face again so I picked up the towel from the work bench and wiped at my face with it. My head was starting to feel better.

"Those young gals I see you walkin' by here with in the mornin'. Them your sisters?"

"Uh-huh. Two of them. There's one more still at home."

This was stupid. Why was I talking to this man? What if he was another bill collector? I changed the subject.

"Is it hard to make things out of wood?"

"Not really. Just takes time. Patience with the small stuff. Like that birdhouse."

He reached on the shelf and pulled down a tiny cedar dwelling. The smallest birdhouse I had ever seen.

"It took me a week to get that hole on the front the right size for the bird to come in. See?"

He handed it to me. The trickle of blood on my face had stopped enough for me to remove the towel and grasp the little structure with both hands.

"Very delicate work," he said, "work" sounding like *wuhk*.

It was delicate. The hole was so small that I wondered what kind of bird could possibly fit though it.

"Where did you learn how to make stuff out of wood?"

He ran a hand through the sparse gray strands on his head.

"I used to work in a lumber yard back home."

"Where's that?"

"Tennessee."

"Oh," I said.

Tennessee, where they killed Martin Luther King Jr. Something in the sound of my voice told him that his answer bothered me.

"You don't like Tennessee?"

I shrugged, not knowing what to say. I kept my eyes peeled for dogs.

"You ever been to Tennessee?"

"No."

He paused for a moment and then grinned.

"Your people told you things about Tennessee, though?"

I averted my eyes and looked down at the birdhouse in my hands.

"It's okay. I understand. Colored folks wasn't treated too good back theah. I suppose they still ain't in some parts. Things is better now. Some. I guess."

I looked at the floor. The sawdust really was everywhere. It smelled good, though. Earthy and natural. Like fresh pine.

"Say," he said. It was his turn to change the subject. "I'll bet your mama is a good cook. She cook you good food?"

"My grandma does. She cooks for us," I said.

He reached up on one of the shelves and pulled down a wooden board. It was smoothly sanded and shaded various hues of brown. It looked to be made of several different kinds of wood. He handed it to me.

"You give your grandma this."

"What is it?"

"It's a cutting board. Made it myself. She can use it for cutting meat. She cooks you meat, right? You ain't one of them odd California folks don't eat meat, is you?"

I giggled.

"No, she cooks meat."

"Good. Then she'll like this. You tell her it's from Josiah up the street. Or Mr. Wilkins if you must."

I stood and looked at the board.

"What's the matter?"

"I really shouldn't take things from strangers. I'll get in trouble."

"We ain't strangers. We neighbors. You can take a gift from your neighbor. Ask your Grandmama. She'll say it's okay."

He grinned again. He had a kind face when he smiled. It had a luminous, angelic quality.

"Okay," I said after giving the matter some serious thought.

"Well, okay," he said, smiling again.

"Thank you again for helping me," I said, again placing the towel on the workbench.

"It was my pleasure," he said, his hand again on my shoulder as we walked to the door.

I grasped the doorknob and I stood there for a moment, a knot in the pit of my stomach.

"Don't worry," he said. "Them boys ain't still around here. I'll stand out front and watch you till you get far enough up the street."

I smiled a relieved smile.

I opened the door and headed up the sidewalk. At least I could use the cutting board as a rock shield. Like Captain America.

After a few minutes, I turned back to see Mr. Wilkins, as good as his word, standing on his doorstep clutching his pitch-fork, watching. As he began to fade into the distance, he waved with his free hand. For the first time, I waved back.

I actually waved back to a man who says "theah."

CHAPTER 19

Waking Up Is Hard to Do Part II

A s are all persons placed on a seventy-two-hour hold under the 5150 ordinance in Alameda County, I was immediately sent to John George Psychiatric hospital in San Leandro for evaluation. I was transferred in a vehicle that was a cross between a police car and an ambulance. It had ambulance colors, but I was confined in the back behind a metal grate that separated me from the driver and his assistant. The Latino driver and his African-American assistant laughed and joked with me during the entire drive. They went on and on about what big fans of mine they were. At least they didn't ask me for autographs.

As shocking as it may be, I was not in the mood for joking. I wanted to go home. I wanted to forget that the whole incident had ever happened. As sad, sick, and depressed as I was, I was more concerned about the stigma that accompanies the revelation of mental illness. If it ever got out that I had been sent to a psychiatric hospital, my world would be over. I don't know why I cared. Had I been successful with my little exhaust fume exercise, it would have all been over anyway—the big difference being that in that case, I wouldn't have been around to know about it.

My home, which was right off of the freeway, lay directly between Highland and John George hospitals.

"Hey guys," I said as we approached my exit. "I live right up ahead. How about just dropping me off at home?"

They laughed.

"You are *so* funny," the assistant said, slapping his thigh.

I was not kidding.

"Really guys, it's not even out of the way. Just drop me off here at home. I'll even pay you for your trouble. Say, a hundred bucks each. Just let me run in the house and get it."

Again they burst out laughing.

"I love that joke you did when I saw you open for Lionel Richie at the Paramount," the driver said. "The one about why gay guys should be allowed in the army."

"I never heard you do that one," the assistant added.

"Hey," the driver said, "why don't you do it for us?"

He was talking about a controversial routine I had performed on the military's "Don't Ask, Don't Tell" policy. I posed the question: If nobody's asking and nobody's telling, how does the army find out who is gay? Is there a clandestine interview? Some kind of a sneaky, verbal Rorschach test? A covert word association game that the recruit doesn't even know he's engaged in? Is there a quiz that they give the new recruits in order to evaluate them for homosexuality? Is it an interview designed to trip them up in order to reveal their "true colors"?

"Your name?"

"John Smith."

"Your age?"

"Eighteen."

"What do you think of Bette Midler?"

It was controversial because army vets and those with military ties in the audience sometimes got upset. I liked performing the bit for just that reason. Tom Sawyer, the former owner of Cobb's Comedy Club in San Francisco and one of my comedy mentors, always told me that unless you're pissing off 20 percent of your audience, you're not doing comedy correctly.

"Come on," the driver said. "Do the joke for us."

"If I do, will you take me home?" I was desperate. Frantic. They laughed again.

"Do the routine for us. It's funny."

I was willing to do anything and everything to just erase that night. I would do whatever I could to obliterate this horrific moment from my memory forever. I would go home, climb into bed, and go to sleep. When I woke up the next morning, it would all have been just a bad dream. What was it Scrooge said in *A Christmas Carol* when first encountered by the ghost of his dead partner, Jacob Marley? The apparition was "only a bit of undigested potato." That's what this nightmare was. Something I ate. If I had to perform for these clowns to go home, fine. I'd dance like a puppet on a string and sing for my supper.

"How many pushups can you do in a minute?" I said in my military voice launching into the bit.

"A hundred."

"Does a wicker basket belong on the table or on the wall?"

"On the wall."

"Mmm hmm," I said, stroking my chin. The driver swerved slightly as he doubled over in laughter. Good, I was winning over the audience. I was going home. I continued.

"What is the motto of the United States Marine Corps?"

"Semper fi, sir."

"Are the socks I'm holding in my hand green or teal?"

Snot flew out of the assistant's nose as he snorted and guffawed. We were fast approaching my exit. It was now a little more than a quarter mile away. I kept the jokes coming.

"Who is the Commander in Chief of the United States Armed Forces?"

"The President of the United States, sir."

"Which movie did Barbra Streisand make first, *Funny Girl* or *Funny Lady?*"

"*Funny Girl.* She only did *Funny Lady* because she was under studio contract."

"Mmm hmm," I said again, stroking my chin as I pantomimed the military interrogator frenetically scribbling in an imaginary notebook.

The driver almost sideswiped a minivan in the next lane as he convulsed in an involuntary surge of hilarity. Tears began to stream down his cheeks.

"Stop," he managed to cough through his chortle. "You're killing me."

I continued.

"If we accept you, what exactly will you be required to protect, preserve, and defend?"

"The constitution of the United States, sir."

"From whom?"

"All enemies foreign or domestic."

"What song did Judy Garland introduce in the film *Meet Me in St. Louis?*"

"That would be 'Have Yourself a Merry Little Christmas.' Want me to sing a few bars?"

The assistant's seatbelt unsnapped as he convulsed forward in his seat, laughing wildly out of control.

"Who were the allies of the United States during the Second World War?"

"Britain and Russia."

"Which countries comprised the Axis powers?"

"Germany, Italy, and Japan."

"If assigned to arctic duty, would you be willing to wear an all-white uniform?"

"Not after Labor Day, sir."

"Stop," the driver pleaded in hysterics. "Stop. I can't breathe. I can't breathe."

"Okay, guys," I said, "I'm up next. Let's drop me off, huh? I'll direct you."

They laughed again.

"I'm serious now, fellas."

They continued laughing.

"Teal," the driver chuckled, losing his composure again. "I love it."

He zoomed past my exit.

"You're missing it," I yelled. My wrought up frustration was boiling to the surface. I felt myself losing control.

"You're missing it!" I said again. This time I'm screaming. Good, Brian. Scream at them. That'll show them you're sane.

"Please. It's right here, pull over. Please take me home. Please."

They ignored me.

"I want to go home." I burst into sobs. "I want to go home."

Now, the tears were rolling down *my* cheeks.

"Please," I whispered. "Please take me home."

The levity had suddenly evaporated from the vehicle. The driver shook his head and focused his vision intently on the road. The assistant looked at me. His eyes, which had only a moment before been watery from laughter, were now sad and compassionate. I watched out the rear window as my exit faded into the distance.

At John George, I was placed in an office where, after a long wait, a Middle-Eastern man in a white coat entered.

Great, men in white coats. I was fucked.

I thought of straightjackets, which led me to think about Houdini. It appeared that the great escape artist was on my mind a lot that evening. I remembered seeing a picture of him once taken in the 1920s in Oakland. In it, Houdini was suspended upside down from the highest peak of the *Oakland Tribune* Tower in a straightjacket, a throng of onlookers gaping up, slack jawed from the street. If he fell, it would mean certain and sudden death, yet his face didn't show the slightest bit of concern. There was a cockiness in his eyes. It was as if he didn't have a care in the world. Here he was, risking death for the entertainment and edification of the great unwashed, folks who hadn't even paid to watch, and he was nonchalant, cool, and collected. I wasn't Houdini. I was looking at a straightjacket right here on good old terra firma, and I was scared to death.

The attendant sat down, looked at a file in front of him, and then, without so much as glancing up, asked, "So, what happened?"

I rambled through the same bullshit story I had told the cops. My car was in the driveway. I put it in the garage. I was just listening to music. I forgot to turn off the motor. That's all. It was simple. It was a very logical explanation.

Finally, as he looked up while I continued to speak, I thought, "Great, he's really hearing me. I'm going home."

My hope of freedom was dashed when I noticed that he wasn't looking *at* me, but rather *past* me. I looked over my shoulder at a computer screen with several yellow Post-it notes virtually covering it.

"Now, why are all those notes there and not in the message box?" he said.

"What?"

"Those aren't supposed to be there," he said. "They should be in the message box."

"I'm talking to you!" I screamed.

Here I go again. I was trying to show someone evaluating my psychological condition how sane and harmless I was by screaming. I would be lucky if they didn't give me electric-shock treatments.

"I'm talking to you and you're looking at the fucking computer instead of listening to me? If you're not going to listen to me, then send somebody in here who will."

He nodded his head, got up and left the room. A few minutes later, I was led back out to the transport vehicle. As I was locked in the back, I heard one of the staffers say to the driver, "Washington Hospital."

I was really fucked.

Fremont, California, lies approximately fifteen miles south of San Leandro and about halfway between San Leandro and San Jose. Its claim to fame and principal source of employment for many years was the now-defunct General Motors plant. When GM shut down in the 1980s, the plant was reborn as New United Motors under a deal with Japanese car manufacturers. The "Nummie" plant, as locals call it, and Washington Hospital, were all I knew of the city of Fremont.

Washington Hospital sits in the southern part of the city of Fremont. It is a facility dedicated to mental-health issues. "Hospital dedicated to mental-health issues" is a nice way of saying "nut house." It's where southern Alameda County's 5150s are confined for "further evaluation."

I was familiar with Washington Hospital because of Dana, my first girlfriend. I had met her a few weeks after my high school graduation and fell in love with her almost instantly. Well, at least, what you think is love when you're eighteen. She was a year younger and about as opposite of me as one could get. She was white, with short red hair and green eyes, and came from a blue-collar Fremont family. Like most laborers living in Fremont at the time, her father worked at the auto plant.

Like most seventeen-year-olds, Dana felt alienated from the world, but her sense of alienation was extreme. So was mine. I think this was what drew us together. What I was soon to find out was that Dana had issues beyond mere societal detachment. She had just been released from Washington Hospital a few weeks before I met her.

At school one beautiful Monday morning, Dana politely excused herself from history class, walked into the girls' bathroom, entered one of the stalls, sat down on the toilet lid, pulled out a razor blade, and proceeded to slit her wrists. As she watched the blood trickle down her arms, she dipped in her index finger, a macabre fountain pen making use of gruesome ink, to write a scarlet message on the wall. "I Hate Mondays."

Boy, can I pick them? Because of the severity of her self-inflicted injuries, Dana spent more than the requisite seventy-two hours in the hospital, and was confined for a few weeks. She'd hated Washington and told me horror stories about the place. I was heading into a scene right out of *One Flew Over the Cuckoo's Nest*.

At Washington, I was again led out of the ambulance/squad car into an office for evaluation. I again cooled my heels for several minutes until another white-coated man (this attendant was white . . . I was *really, really* fucked) came in to chat with me. Unlike the attendant at John George, this guy actually listened to my bullshit. He looked me in the eyes. Every few seconds he nodded his head sympathetically. In a calm, concerned voice, he asked me a few questions about my story.

"So if you were just listening to music, why did you have

the motor running? Why not just turn the ignition key until the battery comes on?"

Hey, he's using logic. What kind of bullshit is this?

"I . . . uh . . . didn't want to run down my battery," I stammered. "I don't have jumper cables."

Yeah, that sounded good.

"A Miata has a manual transmission, doesn't it? You don't need jumper cables if your battery runs down. You can push start it."

Damn. More logic.

"I didn't know that."

"Did you know that breathing in exhaust fumes in a closed garage could kill you?"

"Now you tell me."

He laughed. Maybe I was getting out of there.

"You know," he said, "I'm going to recommend that we keep you here."

"What? Why? I told you it was an accident."

He put his hand on my shoulder.

"My friend, there are some things going on with you. Some very serious things. Some things that you are going to have to deal with or there will be a next time. Next time, you might not be so lucky."

I started to cry again.

"It was an accident."

"Think about me for a minute," he said smiling. "How do you think I'd feel if I let you go home and then later you hurt yourself? Permanently hurt yourself?"

I didn't say anything. I looked at my lap.

"I got kids to feed," he said. "I don't want to look for another job. That's a pain in the ass." He smiled. It was a warm, friendly smile.

"Stay here. It'll be okay. Use the time to try and sort some things out. There are people here who can talk to you, people who will help you, if you'll let them."

I nodded, resigning myself to my fate.

"It will be okay," he said before getting up and leaving me in the office.

After giving the admitting nurse the necessary information, I was led to the ward where they keep the 5150s. I had my own room, which was nice, and I could come and go as I pleased. The one thing I couldn't do was leave the ward. A large locked door prevented me from doing that. I was told that I would be evaluated again in the morning and, if necessary, yet again the following day, until I was no longer deemed a threat to "myself or others."

What "others"? I hadn't been a threat to "others" (sisters excepted, of course) in my life. While I found this entire situation embarrassing, frustrating, and demoralizing, I found the implication that I was a "threat to others" downright insulting. Here we go yet again. Even when I quietly slipped away to off myself in the privacy of my own garage, I was still "the threatening black man." I was still viewed as a danger to somebody else. I can't win for losing.

I couldn't sleep. The first twelve hours I spent pacing. I walked an inside track I had created from my room, down the hall, past the nurses' station and the television room to the big locked door and then back again. My eyes stayed fixed on the hideous, plaid carpet that covered the entire floor. Back and forth I paced, avoiding all eye contact with anyone for fear of being recognized. I had been coming into a quarter of a million Bay Area homes, five days a week for over five years. I didn't want anybody there to make that connection.

I put myself in a kind of self-hypnosis to block out the screams of a young woman in restraints, the incoherent babbling of a street person, and the sobs of a teenage girl. As I walked, I thought. I thought about the apartment complex. I thought about the humiliations. I thought about the cops and Sylvester and the kids in the car that first day. All of that pain hidden for all of those years finally, relentlessly rising to the surface. Mostly, I thought about Mom. Why did you do this to me, Mom? Why did you fuck me up and then leave before I was mature enough to deal with this stuff?

After a while, one of the nurses finally got a clue that I was struggling and offered me something to help me sleep. I took a pill and headed back to my room. My head hit the pillow and I drifted off, wondering if I were dead. In Catholic school, they taught us that suicides don't go to heaven or hell but purgatory, to face the same problems that pushed them over the edge in the first place. Again and again, the same shit, in perpetuity. Did I die in the garage and get sent to purgatory? Was I being punished? Would I spend all eternity hassled by cops, called racial epithets by strangers, berated by those who share my complexion, and at the same time shouldering the blame for their transgressions? Would I spend the rest of all time abandoned by those who were supposed to love me and take care of me? Was this my destiny? Was this my Catholic fate?

I found my mom's diary from the 1970s a few years back. In it she wrote, "I don't want to die, ever. Leave this white world for the infinity and indignity of a white heaven? No thanks."

My last thoughts before I drifted off into slumber were: "Was she right? Is heaven white?"

I was released from the hospital about forty-eight hours later. It was a good sign. They didn't keep me for the whole seventy-two. While I was there I learned some very interesting things. For example, I found out that it's against the law to commit suicide. Isn't that the most ridiculous thing you've ever heard? In the state of California, *it's illegal to commit suicide!* What's the penalty? Death?

It should be against the law to *fail* at committing suicide. The cops should come and say, "You can't even do this shit right. We're taking you in. You're dangerous. You're gonna hurt somebody."

CHAPTER 20

Mr. Ware

"Real estate men in San Leandro conveniently do not show homes to black people. A few years ago, a family on our block listed with a black real estate broker. Well, somebody called the president of our homeowners' association, who in turn called our city councilman, who in turn called a white real estate broker, who then called the black broker who agreed not to show the home to blacks."

—Mrs. Durlyn Anema, community activist. November 1969.

It was a week after Mr. Wentworth broke into our apartment, and Grandma drove me into Palo Alto to my mother's attorney's office. Once we got into the city, I could tell how different Palo Alto was from San Leandro. It was just as clean and the faces I saw walking along the tree-lined streets were just as white, but the homes we passed were palatial. Some of them looked like they were right out of the opening credits of *The Beverly Hillbillies*. I started to look for "swimming pools and movie stars." We eventually made our way to a gleaming office building where Grandma parked the Malibu and ushered me in.

I walked into the outer office and was instantly amazed. It was the nicest office I had ever been in. There was art on the walls and shiny wood furniture. Everywhere I looked there were lawyers and secretaries running back and forth. White lawyers and white secretaries. Grandma walked up to one of them, a pretty brunette typing furiously at her desk on an IBM Selectric.

"We here to see Mr. Ware."

"Oh," the brunette crooned. "You must be Mrs. Arbee."

She smiled at me like a kindergarten teacher greeting a nervous five-year-old on the first day of school.

"And I'll bet you're Brian," she said. "Mr. Ware is waiting for you. Go right in."

Grandma took a seat in the outer office as I followed the chipper *Romper Room* lady inside. When I entered, I realize that it was even nicer in there. The carpet was a thick, lush brown. The walls were wood-paneled a deep reddish brown. It reminded me of the "studies" that all white dads on old TV sitcoms had.

"Bud, I'd like to talk to you. Step into my study, please."

In this office, there was leather furniture. In the middle of the room sat a large mahogany desk. Seated behind the desk was a man. He was wearing an expensive suit tailored perfectly to fit his lean, athletic frame. I noticed that he had his jacket off and that he was wearing cuff links. Gold cuff links. His shoes were so shiny that the light they reflected almost blinded me. He looked professional. Just sitting quietly behind his desk, he had a commanding presence. I had never seen anyone like this man. Like this black man.

"I'm Jim Ware," he said, rising to greet me and grasping my hand in a firm, viselike grip. "And I'll bet you'd like a Coke."

"Do you have any root beer?" I asked.

He pressed a button on his intercom. The chirpy voice of the brunette blared through the box.

"Yes, Mr. Ware?"

"Marjorie, my client would like some root beer. Would you bring one in, please?"

"Right away, Mr. Ware," came the crackled radio response.

Wow! He tells white people what to do!

The secretary came in and left the soda. As I sipped, Mr. Ware asked me a barrage of questions. They came fast and furious. It was as if I only heard his voice. I was sure that I was responding, but my utterances were unimportant in contrast to the timbre of his words. They seemed to seek information, yet impart comfort, alliance, and camaraderie all at the same time.

"How long was Mr. Wentworth in the apartment?"

"What did he say when you caught him?"

"Do you think that you could be a witness?"

"No, son. That's a Jehovah's Witness."

"Do you think that you can tell what it is that you saw?"

"Well, you are a very brave young man."

I was completely and totally in awe. Here was an intelligent, articulate black man and he had . . . respect. No one would ever accuse this man of drowning a cat.

"Mr. Ware," I said. "Can I ask you something? How come you're a lawyer? I mean, why did you become one?"

He got a faraway look in his eyes as he stared off into space. He was quiet for a minute. Dead air. Did I say something wrong?

"My brother," he finally said. "He died. Well, he was killed."

My stomach started to do somersaults. I have an incredible knack for saying the wrong thing. He was so in tune to me already that he sensed my distress.

"It's okay, son. It was a long time ago," he comforted. "A lifetime ago," he said, his eyes losing focus again, running a film in his head that he'd seen a thousand times. The words spilled out of him as he watched his movie and interpreted for the visually impaired.

"September, 1963. I was sixteen and Virgil, that's my little brother, was just thirteen. It started out such a nice Sunday. Warm. Indian summer in Birmingham."

He snapped back to the present.

"Your grandmother's from there, isn't she? And your mom? Really? I've never been to Rhode Island."

He watched his mental movie screen again.

"Anyway, Virgil, our other brother Melvin, and I had just cut a deal to share a paper route. You see, we had it all figured out. We'd divide it amongst us three ways, that way it would take no time at all after school every day. Then, we were gonna pool our money and get a car. Nothing new. Nothing fancy, but ours. All ours.

"Now, Melvin and I had old bikes, you know, good enough to deliver papers with. All we needed to get started now was a bike for Virgil. So, that Sunday after church, Virgil hopped on my handle bars and we headed on up the road toward Docena. We had an uncle up there who owned a scrap yard. We figured we could at least find the makings of a bike, if not a usable one.

"What we didn't know was that earlier that morning across town the Sixteenth Street Baptist Church had been bombed and four little girls, not much younger than us, had been killed."

He shook his head with a combination of disgust and regret.

"All hell's breaking loose, and we're headed for the junk-yard."

He ran a knuckle under his right eye in anticipation of a tear. It didn't come. He cleared his throat and looked at me, trying to be measured in his emotion. Trying to maintain his presence, keeping his personal power.

"Virgil was happy, giddy. You see, he figured that once he

got a car, he'd be getting girls. So I'm teasing him. I'm saying, 'Come on, Virgil. If they don't like you walking, what makes you think they're gonna like you driving?' He says, 'I'll bet I get more girls than you do!' You know, we're carrying on like this as a little red motorbike moves our way from up ahead. As it passes, Virgil falls off of my handlebars and into a ditch on the side of the road.

"I jump off the bike and run over to him. I say, 'Hey Virgil, you all right?' He looks at me with those eyes. I still remember those eyes. They looked right through you, you know? He looks at me and says, 'I think I've been shot.' "

I held my breath. My heart was in my throat.

"I never heard any gunfire. Just the sound of the motorbike as it passed with two white boys on it. They had a little confederate flag on the back flapping in the breeze.

"I cradle Virgil in my arms. He's shaking and trembling. His right cheek is covered in blood. I wipe it. It's warm and sticky."

His voice cracked. His soul, his very core, emerged. It was a large, gaping wound. I wished at that moment that I was one of those empaths I had seen on *Star Trek*, so that I could heal him with my touch. Take away his pain.

"You'll be all right, Virgil," he muttered, the tears finally welling up in his eyes. "Just quit trembling and you'll be fine. Just quit trembling. It'll be okay. Just stop trembling."

He hung his head onto his chest, his spirit broken.

"And then, he stopped and went limp in my arms. Just like that. One minute we're laughing and joking about girls, the next, my brother's lying dead in a ditch."

He straightened his tie in an attempt to regain his composure, to return from that tortured place. He poured a glass of water from the copper-colored pitcher resting on his desk and sipped slowly, medicinally.

"They caught the boys who did it. Eagle Scouts, if you can believe that. On their way home from a white-power meeting or something when they came upon us. The proverbial wrong place at the wrong time."

He picked up the water glass and drained it. It revitalized him. He grabbed the pitcher and filled the glass again. Pain must be dehydrating.

"There was a trial," he continued. "But this was Birmingham. An all-white jury found them guilty of manslaughter. You know what that is, son?"

I shook my head.

"Manslaughter means that those boys didn't mean to kill my brother. Two bullets in him and they didn't 'mean' to do it. The judge gave them probation."

He repeated the word, shaking his head, hoping that saying it again would make the events less real.

"Probation. You got more time in Birmingham for killing a dog."

He sipped from the glass again. This time the gesture was a punctuation mark, giving impact to his words.

"My mother collapsed in the courtroom. Virgil was her baby. And me, I had a decision to make. I could hate, or I could fight. For justice. The justice my brother never got."

I was just a little kid, but this was the saddest story I had ever heard in my life. I don't think that I could have been more touched, more moved, more deeply and personally affected by what he had told me if . . . it had actually been true.

As it turns out, Virgil Ware *did* die in a ditch in Birmingham in September of 1963. And he did die in the arms of his brother James Ware—only not *this* James Ware. This James Ware was no relation, but he told this story and used it to advance his career for years . . . all the way up to Federal Court judge.

Twenty-five years later, President Clinton would nominate him for the 9th Circuit U.S. Court of Appeals, a straight shot from there to a seat on the U.S. Supreme Court. At that time Virgil Ware's real brother found out what this James Ware had been doing all these years. Judge Ware was humiliated and forced to withdraw from consideration. When I read about this in the papers it blew my mind. An entire reputation for good works down the toilet over a lie, and a lie he didn't even have to tell. Why?

He had meant so much to me as a kid. Here was a vision of what I could be. Here was the encapsulation of my mother's dreams. Work hard and study. Do good works and help people. Be professional and well dressed and articulate and people of all colors will respect you. They'll have to, because you've "earned" it.

As children, Tracie and I used to wish that Mr. Ware was our father. We had fantasies about him marrying our mother and moving us into a big house in Palo Alto where we would have a backyard and a dog and friends. Neighbors would respect us and treat us with regard because our father was a professional man, a man who wore a suit and tie to work and carried a briefcase, a briefcase I would dutifully take into his study for him when he came home from work. In his study, we would have man-to-man talks about life and honor and right and wrong. It would be a study where he would never strangle me or yell at me for cutting my eyes at him.

Why did he do it? Why tell this enormous lie for so many years? Why? He was, and remains to this very day, a good judge who had the respect of his colleagues and of other lawyers, particularly young black lawyers who looked up to him just like I did. Why did he inject himself into somebody else's tragedy? Who was he trying to justify himself to?

Is this what he felt that he had to do in order to be a "genuine black man"?

Was it survivor's guilt? Here he had achieved a position that few black men in this society ever reach. He was a black lawyer at a prestigious law firm in the tony and wealthy enclave of Palo Alto—Stanford University country. He employed white people who were actually subservient to *him*. Was he guilty about that? Did he feel that he had to have had an authentic "black experience" in order to have credibility among white people? Or among black people? It was widely reported that he told this story at conferences and gatherings of legal professionals, bringing his audiences to tears and receiving standing ovations after he described his "brother's" death as fueling his "passion for justice."

When the truth finally did come out, he didn't behave much better initially. At first he claimed that his father had sired another family in Birmingham whom he'd never met and that in that "other family" was a boy named James. This, he said, led him to assume that Virgil Ware was his half-brother. Be that as it may, that's a long way from the mortally wounded boy actually dying in his arms.

Later, after the widespread national condemnation and negative publicity had reverberated all the way to the White House, Judge Ware finally came clean and flew to Birmingham where he apologized to Virgil's brother in person. According to media accounts, the Birmingham Wares were cordial and forgiving. I guess that facing such a tragedy as they had puts the rest of your life in perspective in one way or another.

The question still remains: Why did this educated, talented, well-liked, and respected attorney, this role model, feel the need to usurp someone else's story? Was it to "prove" to black people that, although he was held in lofty esteem now, he had come from humble and tragic beginnings? That he was one of them, despite the tailored suits and ritzy business digs?

There's another possibility. How would you like to come from Birmingham and not have any stories? He *did* come from there, and he *had* lived there in the turbulent 1960s. There were explosions going off all over the place. The national media used to call it "Bombingham." How embarrassing would it be to come from that time and that place and have nothing to tell people?

"I will never forget the Sunday we went to church services, and when it was over . . . we went home. I'll never forget that day!"

Condoleezza Rice came from there at that same time. I read an article someplace that said that the closest she'd come to the Civil Rights movement was when she was a little girl and her father took her downtown when they were trying to desegregate the lunch counter at Woolworth's. They watched as Bull Conner was there with the fire hoses and the police dogs. All of the protesters were there blocking the street as her daddy took her by the hand.

"You see this, Condi?" he asked. "Don't *ever* do this. Come on. You've got an ice-skating lesson."

What is it that makes the racial authenticity of a successful black male in this society suspect? What is it? It really pisses me off when I think about it, because if you go to the street corners of East Oakland or San Francisco's Bay View Hunter's Point district or Detroit or Compton or just about any other urban area with a large, predominantly black population, you'll find all these guys selling crack, and all of these guys with five babies by five different women, none of whom they're supporting and *nobody* is saying that they're not real black men.

What about guys like Sylvester? He abused me. He abused

my mother. He never worked. He never brought money home. He abandoned us. Yet never once in his life did anybody ever accuse him of not being a "genuine black man." Never once was he taken to task for his behavior and accused of racial betrayal. Never once did anyone wag a finger in his face and say, "You're an abusive parasitic piece of shit . . . and, you're not black!"

Is that what the black person who sent me that letter at the radio station expects me to be? Is that the implied requirement of all of those people, both black and white, who have taunted me my entire life? Is that what's expected of me by those who called me an "Oreo" or an "Al Jolson," a white man with a black face? They want me to be Sylvester? Is that what they're telling me? I have to be the worst possible stereotype or I'm not "keeping it real"? Is that what the anonymous letter was all about?

Anonymous letters are such chicken shit. I find them to be both cowardly and frustrating. Cowardly because if you have some criticism, gripe, or complaint you just *have* to make, you should have the guts to stand behind it. Take credit for your belief, don't just throw rocks over a wall where you can't be seen. They're frustrating because you can't respond. You can't defend against the attack.

Ever since I got that letter, I've had this fantasy. I'd take it to Selmark Labs and have the DNA analyzed. The writer would have left his genetic markers when he licked the envelope and the stamp. Then, I'd track down his address and go to his house. I'd politely knock on his door and when he answered, I'd shove the letter in his face. He'd look at me in stunned silence as I then grabbed him by the front of his shirt, got in his face, and said:

"I read your letter and I came here because apparently, I owe you an apology and I wanted to deliver it in person. I want to apologize right here and now for failing to meet your racial expectations. I have evidently let you down in this regard and I'm sorry."

His eyes would then get large, and sweat would form on his brow. He wouldn't be able to believe I found him and that I was actually on his doorstep. I'd pull him closer, so we were standing nose to nose, as I'd say:

"I apologize, truly, I'm sorry that I don't deal drugs. I'm sorry that all of my children were born into wedlock and that I support them. I'm sorry that I help them with their homework and that I don't tell them that getting good grades is 'acting white.'"

He would be squirming now. He would try to back away from me. As he did, I'd grip his shirt tighter and pull him even closer.

"I'm sorry that I don't think that a guy disrespecting women by rhyming about 'bitches and hos' to the sound of a bass guitar is music. I'm sorry that I speak standard English instead of street talk. I'm sorry that I read books for my personal enjoyment. I'm sorry that I'd rather play chess than basketball."

He'd try to say something, stammering a response. I'd cut him off at the knees and shout him down.

"I'm sorry that I won't let my kids walk around with their pants at their knees and their underwear hanging out of their behinds. I'm sorry that when I get a few nickels to rub together, I don't spend them draping myself in gold chains and gold teeth, or buying rims that spin when I'm at a stoplight."

At this point, he would be furiously trying to escape my grasp and slip back into the anonymous safety of his house. His "genuinely black" house. I wouldn't let him. I'd grip his shirt tighter still. I'd scream, my voice bellowing the answer not just for him but for all of those who've made this bullshit charge of blacks who try to live a better life. For all of us who defy stereotype.

"Please forgive me for wanting more and not less. Forgive me for wanting to live in a nice neighborhood where I'm not kept awake at night by gunshots, sirens, and screams. I'm sorry. I'm sorry that I look so shitty in an orange jumpsuit that I'm not going to prison for anybody. I'm sorry that I care more about a 401K than a 187PC. I'm sorry, I'm sorry, *I'M SORRY*."

I'd then let him go. He wouldn't know what to say as I turned and walked down his driveway. As I reached the sidewalk, I'd turn and look at him, still standing in his doorway, trying to recover from the surprise attack.

"I know," I'd say. "I'm still a nigger."

I left Mr. Ware's office that day knowing what I was going to do with the rest of my life. I was going to be a lawyer. But not just a lawyer, a *civil rights lawyer*, just like him. I was going to have a big office and a mahogany desk and a white secretary to bring me root beer at the press of a button. And, I was going to help people. People like my mom.

I was so excited. I couldn't wait to tell my mom that I had a vocation. Grandma hadn't even turned off the motor as I raced out of the car and into the apartment. I flew up the stairs. Without knocking, I flung open Mom's bedroom door.

"Mommy, guess what?" I shouted.

It was then that the stench hit me. The sickening, musky smell of Brut.

Sylvester sat on the corner of the bed. He was wearing an old tank top and a pair of ratty jeans. His head was covered with a hairnet. Nobody will ever bring him root beer.

"Hey son!" he said with a smile. Like we were pals.

"Hey," I managed to get out. It was a surreal moment.

"Come here and give your daddy some sugar."

I walked over to him, leaned down, and kissed him on the cheek, the smell of his cheap cologne making me nauseous. He reached out with his index finger and touched the tip of my nose. His touch was like a posthypnotic suggestion taking me back to the age of five. Back to the bruised nose. Back to my bruised spirit. He thought he was being affectionate. I felt dizzy.

My mother came walking out of the bathroom. She was dressed to go out.

"Oh, hi, honey," she said, all goodness and light. "How'd it go with Mr. Ware?"

"Okay," I muttered, still shell-shocked.

"I see you've talked to your father."

"Uh-huh."

"He's coming home."

CHAPTER 21

The Funk

I n my early days at KGO Radio, I had a very close and dear friend named Duane Garrett. In the summer of 1995, Duane—a big, funny, gregarious fellow—jumped to his death from the Golden Gate Bridge. As in most cases of this type, everyone who knew him was shocked. We hadn't seen it coming. He was a successful entrepreneur, lawyer, radio-talk-show host, and politico. He managed the U.S. Senate campaign of Dianne Feinstein and was a friend and confidant of then–Vice President Al Gore.

Duane was the official historian of the San Francisco Giants and a partner in a large auction house that specialized in rare sports memorabilia. He had a loving wife and two daughters who adored him. His home rested atop a bluff in Marin County and it had a picturesque view of San Francisco and the very bridge that he would one day use to end his life. By all appearances he had it all.

As the wisdom that comes with age teaches us, appearances can be deceiving. After his death, it would come to light that Duane was having serious financial difficulties. His entire monetary situation was a façade, built precariously on a house of cards. A house of cards that was about to come tumbling down.

When you live a life as public as Duane's was, it's a double-edged sword. While your successes, accolades, and accomplishments are lauded to the masses, so are your failures, faults, mistakes, and faux pas. Just as the spotlight magnifies the positive things, it also intensifies and blows out of proportion the negative things. There's an old joke on the subject.

Q. How come all the king's horses and all the king's men couldn't put Humpty Dumpty back together again?
A. Because he fell from such a high place.

As a man who had grown up "the fat kid," who worked his tail off to achieve success and thus had his very self-image tied up in those achievements, the thought of the public humiliation of failure was unbearable for him.

When Duane died, the universal refrain was, "What a selfish thing to do." I disagree. Suicide has nothing to do with selfishness or "taking the easy way out." Suicide is the result of pain. It is the culmination of an anguish so great that you will do *anything* to make it stop.

Imagine that you have a blade sticking in your shoulder. Once the blade has penetrated your flesh to the bone, it's being twisted—slowly, excruciatingly. You can't see straight. You can't think straight. All you know is the pain and you don't know how to get the blade out of your arm. If you were in that position and somebody said, "You can make it stop. Just drink this bottle of strychnine," trust me, you'd use your free arm to grab the strychnine. That's why people take their own lives.

Fortunately, most people have the resources to remove the blade, be it family support, therapeutic support, or spiritual support. They have a coping mechanism by which they can make the hurting stop or, at the very least, find a way of dealing with it. It is those who lack such systems who commit suicide. The truly sad thing is that lots of those people do indeed have resources to help them. They don't realize it because of isolation, the clouding of the mind that accompanies depression, or, as in Duane's case and mine, pride. Pride doth indeed go before a fall.

Had Duane Garrett told his friends that he was in trouble, had he confided in the multitude of people he had helped and nurtured over the years, had he simply asked for help, there isn't a person who knew him who wouldn't have done something to assist in rectifying his situation. Any one of us would have pulled the blade out for him. That's the true tragedy.

There were people who would have gladly taken out my blade, too. All I had to do was ask. My own pride and hubris wouldn't allow it. I was a lone wolf, the only one of my kind in the universe. There was nobody I could turn to, nobody I could trust but me. Not my wife, not my friends, not Grandma or my sisters. If there was a problem, I would find a way of dealing with it for myself, by myself. Anything short of that would have been a sign of weakness. I had spent a lifetime learning that the world is an ocean full of sharks looking for black meat. The second I showed myself to be a wounded animal in their waters would be the very second that they'd devour me.

The interesting thing is that this attitude makes me more of a "genuine black man" than I realized. Black people aren't depressed. They don't talk about it or deal with it. They can't show weakness and they damned sure can't lie on a shrink's couch lamenting their woes. If they can't take the blade out by themselves, damn it, they'll leave the motherfucker right where it is.

During my worst days, I would take Duane's walk. I'd park at Vista Point by the Golden Gate Bridge and walk to the spot behind one of the towers where I figured he must have jumped. It's a place that can't be seen by passing motorists. I'd stand there, sometimes for hours, looking over the railing, crying and pondering my life. I thought of going over the side many times but it was just too damned high. My fear of heights trumped my fear of life. Eventually, I'd make my way back to my car and head home or to the TV station to prepare for the next morning's wacky antics. The tears of a very sad clown.

For me, every slight, every indignity, every reminder that I was "not like the others" was a twist of the blade. I ignored it and used mental tricks to block out the pain. I bit down on the bullet as long as I could until I finally reached for the strychnine.

CHAPTER 22

There's Always Something

"I had an opportunity on one or two occasions to present an offer. During the presentation, the broker—I learned later that he was giving signs to the owner as to when to get back and when to talk. We were supposed to have gone in to see the owner before the others. I got there a few minutes early, and when I got there, he was coming out of the owner's house and he had apparently been in and told her to reject my offer. And while I was in there, he would rub his ear or rub his nose, pull his hair, use his left or his right hand, you know, to indicate to the owner. The reason I know this to be a fact is because I cooperated with him on an Oakland property later and he told me these were the kinds of things he did when he wanted the seller to react."

—Ray Cullen, Oakland Realtor, on trying to help
black buyers purchase a San Leandro home, November, 1971

In spite of the guerilla war that was being waged against us after Mom filed her lawsuit, we tried to live a life as normal as possible. We tried to pretend, or at least I did, that we were just like everybody else. We tried to do the same things that other people did. That meant going to church and school, doing our chores and keeping our apartment neat, having family dinners and holidays together. Just like normal people. Just like everybody else. The problem was that we weren't like everybody else. I certainly wasn't, and no matter how hard I tried to blend in, there would be some force to remind me. Something to keep me in my place.

It was Christmastime and I had been saving my allowance and money from extra chores and odd jobs for weeks. Through my efforts, I had managed to amass the princely sum of twenty-four dollars to go shopping for Christmas presents for my family. It had gone pretty far, that twenty-four bucks. I got a hurricane lamp for Mom. I didn't know what she'd use it for because we didn't have hurricanes in California, but it was pretty, it was glass, and it was six bucks. I got some strawberry-shaped pin cushions for Grandma, some jacks for Tracie, and a doll that wet herself for Delisa.

All of my finds were neatly tucked away in the old wooden shipping chest I kept under my bed. The chest was cool. I had won it in a card game from one of the kids in the apartments. One of the handful who would actually play with me. We played a two-hour game of War, me wagering my comic collection against his wooden chest. It was the first time in my life that I had ever won anything. Best of all, even after I beat him, the kid still played with me. He didn't get mad, didn't call me the "n" word or anything. Things were looking up.

I had a whopping four dollars of shopping money left and one last present to buy, this one for my sister Tonya, the baby of the family. I had decided that the best place to find her something worthwhile (and within my budget) was the local Gemco store. Gemco was a chain of discount stores like Target and Wal-Mart. They had everything from clothes and albums to cameras and telescopes. They also had a great (and inexpensive) toy department.

I was a big fan of the Oakland Raiders. I had met Bob

Hudson, who was their special team captain, and he gave me a silver and black Raiders beanie that had been permanently attached to my head for weeks. I wore it everywhere. Even to bed. I was proudly wearing it as I walked into the local Gemco store that day.

I walked from aisle to aisle, making my way through the throng of bustling white people. I imagined that we were all there on the same mission: finding presents for our little sisters. We were all doing the same thing at the same time. We were the same. We were alike. We were all normal.

I browsed carefully, looking for the best way to utilize my four dollars. "Utilize" was a word I had just learned. It was in one of my Hardy Boys books. Frank and Joe utilized a rope to help their friend Chet, who was hanging from a cliff. I utilized "utilize" every chance that I got. Mom said it made me sound literate.

There were great toys everywhere, Lite-Brite, G.I. Joe, Rock 'Em Sock 'Em Robots, and of course an entire aisle devoted to Barbie. All kinds of Barbies but all white except for Malibu Barbie, who had a tan. (I have never understood the concept of tanning. If white people dislike black people so much, why do they spend so much time trying to make themselves darker?) I could afford a Malibu Barbie; it was the cheapest. The darkest one was the least expensive. Go figure. But it worked for me. After I paid, I might even have enough left over to buy a comic book at 7-Eleven on my way home.

I was contemplating the purchase when I noticed the man. He was wearing a white dress shirt, brown corduroy jacket, a bad tie, and a worse haircut. I realized he had been near me since shortly after I entered the store. Sometimes he was right beside me. Sometimes he was right on my heels.

Other times, I'd be in an aisle checking something out and after a few minutes, he appeared out of nowhere looking at something on the shelf next to me. He was looking for a present for his little sister, just like me. Another comrade in normalcy.

As I picked up the Barbie doll and studied it, he approached me directly. Without saying a word, he pulled out a leather wallet with a shiny golden badge attached to it.

Cool, I thought. *Just like* Baretta*!*

Grandma and I liked to watch *Baretta* on Friday nights. Baretta was great. He fought crime and he had a trained bird that sat on his shoulder. Best of all, when he busted somebody, he'd bore them to death with a lecture before taking them in. As if jail by itself wasn't enough to get the message across.

"Hold it right there, man, I'm the heat," he'd say. "Now you messed up, you rummy, but that's okay because that's the way of the world and that's the way things go, see. It's like my old man used to say, 'The truth's sometimes like a dead skunk in the street, man. You can walk away from it all you want, but that don't make it stink no less.' You can take that to the bank. You can cash interest on it, too."

The poor crook's going, "Take me to jail! I confess! Give me the gas chamber, just shut up!"

I wondered if San Leandro had cops like Baretta. I wondered if any of them had trained birds.

"I'm store security," he said as I stared at his badge.

He was not Baretta. His badge looked like the one I'd sent for out of *Boy's Life* magazine, the one in the ad next to the Sea Monkeys, the fake puke, and the pepper-flavored gum.

"Yes, sir?" I answered. Mom always said to be polite. No matter what, she said, "Always be a gentleman."

"I need you to come with me, please."

I was a little bit scared, and a little bit intimidated. I followed him through the store, past my shopping peers, and then through a door in the back. It was painted white. A desk covered with papers sat in the middle of the room with a chair behind it and one in front of it. The manager's office. He motioned for me to sit in the chair in front of the desk as he moved around behind it.

"May I please see some identification?" he said.

What was it with white people and ID in this town? I pulled out my wallet. It was tan leather with the head of a horse embroidered on it. I undid the brown zipper that sealed it shut.

"Um, I have my library card and a detective's card I got from the *Hardy Boys Detective Handbook*."

I threw in the Hardy Boys card, thinking he'd be impressed. Like he was going to say, "Oh, you're a colleague. It's okay. You can go." Wrong. He gestured toward the desk.

"Please empty your pockets and place the contents on the desk."

"Huh?"

"Please take everything out of your pockets and put it on the desk. Start by cleaning out the wallet."

I didn't know why he wanted me to do this, but I opened my wallet and took out the library and Hardy Boys cards. In the money compartment, I took out four one-dollar bills and my Boy Scouts card. I placed them on the desk in front of him.

"Now your pockets," he said.

I reached into my pockets and took out three dimes, two nickels, seven pennies, the Master padlock I used for my American Flyer bicycle, and three metal pull-tabs from Coke cans that I found on the walk to the store. I was trying to make the world's biggest chain of soda-can pull-tabs. The one I had at home was almost as long as I was tall.

He eyed the stuff and poked through it with a ballpoint pen he picked up from the desk top.

"Is that it?"

"Yes, sir."

"Pull your pockets inside out."

I reached in and pulled my pockets out, the fabric flopping at my sides like the ears of a cocker spaniel.

"Let me see your jacket."

Didn't he ever say "please"? Why wasn't he being a gentleman like Mom said? I took off my navy blue windbreaker and handed it to him. He reached into the pockets. The first was empty as he pulled it out. The second unleashed a torrent of dried snot paper. I was just getting over a cold and I forgot to throw it away.

He frowned as he brushed the dirty tissues into the wastebasket adjacent to the desk. He poked through my things some more with the pen, opened my wallet, making sure that it was empty, and then announced, "You can go."

He folded his arms and lorded over me as I slowly picked up my treasures and put them back into my pockets. I skipped filling my wallet and instead stuffed the dollar bills and cards into my pockets. I wanted to get out of there. I felt . . . funny. My stomach was queasy. My face was numb and I was a little woozy. It was like I had a fever. My eyes were watering. I had allergies, but not this time of year. Only in the spring.

As I walked out of the office door, it hit me like a cold burst of winter air. *He thinks I'm a crook.* I was just looking around. I was just trying to find a Christmas present for my baby sister.

I even had money, see? He thought I was a crook. How could he think I'm a crook?

I left the store and I was in a daze. The next thing I knew I was walking in the front door of the apartment. I didn't know how I got there. I didn't remember the walk. Had I run? Flown?

Mom was sitting on the plastic couch. The moment I set foot inside the apartment, she asked, "What's wrong?"

How did she do that? She always knew when something wasn't right with me. Even if I denied it, she knew.

I told her what happened. I told her about the Mailbu Barbie and the man following me and the badge and going into the back room and emptying my pockets and watching the man poke through my stuff. Streams of tears poured out of my eyes and down my cheeks. It was like I was flushing out my soul.

"He thought I was a crook, Mommy," I said. "How can he think I'm a crook? I get good grades. I'm in the scouts. I even have a detective's card. How can he think I'm a crook. I just wanted to buy a present for Tonya. I'm not a crook. I'm not a crook," I sobbed.

My nose was running then. I reached into my jacket pocket for a tissue. They were gone. I remembered the man brushing them into the trash and I sobbed harder.

"I'm an altar boy!" I screamed. "I'm an altar boy."

Suddenly, she was there cradling my head against her breast.

"It's okay, honey. Shh. It's okay."

"Why did he think I was a crook? I earned my money. All of it."

"I know you did, Brian."

"I'm not a crook!"

"I know that."

"Then why did he think that? What did I do?"

"You didn't do anything." She paused and took my face in her hands as she looked into my eyes. Her soft, brown eyes looked sad. "You're a young black male."

"Huh?"

"Some people are always going to look at you as though you're doing something wrong because," her voice cracked, "you're a black man."

"But that's not fair, Mom. It's not fair!"

She pulled me close again and stroked my back.

"I know, honey. I know. It's not fair, but nobody ever promised that things in this world would be fair. It's just . . . the way things are. There will be times in your life when you will be guilty until you prove yourself innocent. There will be times when you will have to work twice as hard to get half as far. There will be times when you will be caused grief and hurt just because you're there. No, it's not fair. It's life."

My sobs were now uncontrollable.

"Then it doesn't matter how hard I try, how hard I try to do good things. It doesn't matter because people will still think I'm a bad person."

She was silent. For the first time in my memory, she actually didn't know what to say. I pushed away from her, my chest heaving, my breath short as my sobs grew greater.

"Black is bad then!" I shouted. "Being black is bad! Why did God make me this way? What did I do? Why is he punishing me? Why? Why?"

She looked at the floor, her eyes filling with tears. I ran up the stairs to my room and slammed the door. In here, I was safe. It was my Fortress of Solitude, just like Superman's. No one could hurt me here. I could be by myself.

I sat on the bed Indian-style, my arms wrapped around my pillow. I lay the side of my head against it as I slowly rocked, back and forth, the pillow absorbing my tears.

"I don't want to be black. I'm not bad. I'm not bad," I whispered, my voice hoarse from crying. "I'm not bad," I said as I drifted off to sleep.

CHAPTER 23

A Kindred Spirit

I sat alone at my double desk as the teacher handed back the English tests that we had taken the previous day. I listened to the cacophony of moans and groans as the other kids looked at their papers, most of them awash in marks of red ink. I thought that it was a fairly easy test. All right, it was a very easy test as far as I was concerned. It was on antonyms. Opposites. Who would know better about opposites than the only black kid in the class?

The teacher smiled as she dropped a test on my side of the double desk. There was some red ink, but not much. The test consisted of a list of twenty words and we were to write the antonyms for them. I had missed two, the opposites of "play" and "walk," for a final grade of 90 percent. It was an A-minus. I knew that the correct answers were "work" and "run" respectively. I had missed them on purpose. In the beginning, I got all 100 percent grades on tests. Usually I was the only one in the class to do so. The other kids would tease me and make fun of me for it. This I didn't need. I stood out enough already. Why give them yet another reason to torment me?

I read in one of my *Superboy* comics where young Clark Kent had a superintellect. He could ace any exam in a breeze. He could even do it at superspeed, finishing it in seconds, if he really wanted to. The problem was that perfect scores would make him stand out, and somebody might figure out his secret identity. They might discover that he really wasn't one of the "normal" kids at Smallville High. They'd learn that, in fact, he wasn't anything like them at all. For this reason, he would always deliberately miss a few answers on each test in order to avoid arousing suspicion. I began to do the same thing.

After the tests were handed back, I looked up to see a young woman from the principal's office standing at the classroom door. I think she was the school secretary. That was my assumption, at least. She was always in there typing. I spent enough time in the principal's office that I should have known. The one constant in most of the fights at school was me; ergo, it was assumed that I was the problem.

The secretary was accompanied by a skinny, blond-haired kid. Although he was not really moving, he looked awkward and gawky as he stood there surveying the room. "Awkward" and "gawky" are two adjectives that I could relate to well. The woman whispered something to the teacher and then left the boy standing there.

"May I have everybody's attention," the teacher said.

The class was so unruly she had to repeat herself twice, each time louder than the time before. Finally, there was silence as all eyes directed their gaze at the boy.

"This is Jon Regan," she said. "He'll be joining our class starting today. Everyone say 'hi.'"

"Hi," we said in a robotic unison.

"I'm sure that everyone will do his or her best to make Jon feel welcome, right?"

"Yes," the class said, politely, mechanically.

"Let's find you a desk," she said as she looked around the room.

I don't know why she made such a production out of it.

There was only one empty seat among the sea of double desks—the one next to me.

"Jon, you sit over there next to Brian."

He ambled over toward my desk. As awkward as he was standing in the doorway, he was even more so as he walked. It was almost like his brain hadn't caught up with the growth of his body, yet. I could relate. Neither had mine.

The boy plopped down next to me. I didn't say anything. I put my head down and studied my 90 percent in order to avoid eye contact. Eventually he introduced himself and I did the same. That was the extent of it. I didn't want to go any further than that. I figured that once he got to know the other white kids, he would join them in my persecution. I had seen it before when new kids had been added to the class. I'd make friends with them and then they'd go through their "don't be friends with the nigger" orientation and that would be that. Why set myself up yet again? It was all about survival now.

We sat next to each other for about a month and communicated little. I pretty much kept to myself. He made friendly overtures, showing me pictures that he'd drawn and trying to strike up conversations. I would smile, but I remained wary. I didn't share much. I certainly didn't tell him anything personal.

Soon, it turned out that I had been wrong about his relationships with the other kids. Like me, he wasn't much of an athlete. He was better at basketball than I was (who wasn't?) and he could kick a ball a little better than I could, but his proficiency was still far behind that of the other kids. He got 100 percent marks on his tests. Unlike me, he had no secret identity to protect. After a while, the kids started to pick on him, too. They called him "reject" instead of Regan. They played tricks on him. At recess, when the kids were choosing up teams, the only thing that saved him from being picked last was the fact that I was there. I could tell that it hurt his feelings, but he took it in stride.

One morning, I came in to find a small white envelope on my side of our desk. It was an invitation to Jon's birthday party on Saturday. He was turning nine.

"Do you think you can come?" he asked me, anxious.

"I don't know. I'll try. I have to ask my mom," I muttered. My answer was short, terse. The whole invitation was problematic.

I didn't really want to go. He had invited just about the entire class. Why would I want to spend a Saturday with the same kids who picked on me and refused to play with me during the week? On the other hand, no one had invited me to a birthday party since we had moved there. It was nice to be included. I eventually relented and decided to go.

Saturday came and I headed to Jon's house. As I daydreamed on the half mile walk down the street, I suddenly I felt a knot in the pit of my stomach. I was a little nauseous. I felt myself starting to get a little sad. Then I looked around and realized where I was. I was in the spot I had run to when the kids chased me that first Saturday in San Leandro. The boys in the "rebels" jackets. I was standing where the cop had frisked me and put me in the police car. I hadn't been there since that day, but it was right on the route to Jon's house.

I continued the walk feeling a little blue, eventually knocking at Jon's front door, where his mom answered. Whereas most of the mothers of my classmates appeared to be older, she was a younger mom, like mine. Her smile was warm and she was friendly. I went into the house, which was all decorated with balloons and streamers. Jon stood in the front room with his two little sisters and his little brother. He invited me to sit on the floor and play a board game with him until the other kids arrived and we could start the party.

We played a game. And then another. And then another as we waited for the other kids to get there. Forty-five minutes later, no one else had arrived. It hit me at that moment that no one else was coming. I started to feel sad again, but this time for Jon. I realized that he was just like me. He was an outsider. He didn't fit in. He was a nice guy and he was smart. And like me, he was different. An idea hit me.

I thought to myself, "Maybe we can be different together."

Jon's mother started the party. It was just Jon, his siblings, and me. We played games and we ate and we laughed. It was the best time I'd ever had at a birthday party. I stayed long after the party was supposed to end and it was wonderful. I wanted to cry, but this time it was because I was happy. I wasn't the only one of my kind anymore. I wasn't alone. I had a buddy who liked comic books and the Hardy Boys. He wrote great stories and he drew the best pictures I had ever seen a kid draw. He got good grades and wasn't ashamed of it. Best of all, he didn't look like me and it didn't matter. It didn't even occur to him.

Now, when my mom said, "Brian, why don't you go out and play," I had someplace to go and somebody to play with. For the first time, I had a friend. For the first time in a long time I didn't feel lonely.

The next week's English test would be on synonyms: words that are the same. Sameness. Similarity. Resemblance.

"I'll do pretty well on this test," I thought. "I think I'm going to answer *all* of the questions correctly, too."

CHAPTER 24

A Gesture

It turned out that what I had done in the garage that night did not rise to the level of a suicide attempt. This little intern at the hospital told me so.

"Oh, guys don't do stuff like you did. Guys shoot themselves and jump out of windows."

Great, I survived so she could emasculate me. Thank you very much. I appreciate that. It felt like those singsong taunts of third graders.

"You commit suicide like a girl!"

How do black men do it? Oh yeah, they reach for their wallet during a traffic stop.

It turns out that what I had done that night was technically considered to be "a gesture." A gesture? I thought that a gesture was sending flowers or holding my cheek in the palm of my hand like Jack Benny. I didn't know that it included asphyxiation. You learn something every day, don't you?

They also told me that I might, just might, be suffering from depression. Gee, do you think? I don't know. Usually, there's nothing like sheer bliss to put me in the mood for some carbon monoxide gas.

I went to a psychiatrist who put me on medication. It was a cocktail of Wellbutrin and Buspar, to manage my chemical imbalance and elevate my serotonin levels, and some Remeron so that I could sleep. The physician said I'd have to take the drugs for two years and that it would be a month before I had enough of the medicine in my system to be effective. A month before I noticed any difference in how I was feeling. A month. A month in a deep, dark pit with no windows and no light. A month of lying on the couch without the energy to move.

As I lay there, I could hear my kids out on the front lawn playing. They had been so good through all of this. It was decided that they wouldn't be told what had transpired. They were used to me leaving for out-of-town performances. They just assumed I was out doing a gig when I was in the hospital.

When I came home, I did my best to put on a happy face. I thought I was keeping them out of it, but I couldn't fool Carolyn. She was eight years old and very much like me. She would look at me, a stiff smile plastered on my face, and ask, "Daddy, why do you look so sad?"

Their mother became distant and evasive. She dealt with my depression by avoiding the situation entirely, spending less and less time at home, retreating to a local biker bar with new-found friends. I guess we all anesthetize however we have to.

As I lay on the couch listening to the kids laughing and giggling, playing Twister, I sank lower. I wanted so much to go out and play with them, but I couldn't. I couldn't even move.

CHAPTER 25

The Man of the House

I came home from school and the apartment appeared to be empty. I reasoned that Mom and Grandma must still be at work and my sisters were probably still at school. That left the question, where was Sylvester? Actually, that was always the question.

At that moment, a craving took over my body. I wanted a great big salad bowl filled to the brim with Cap'n Crunch. Isn't that the best after school snack in the world? It's sweet and crunchy and it shreds the shit out of the roof of your mouth. What more can a kid ask for?

I opened the wooden door of the cupboard. Just as I reached for a bowl, I was startled by a sharp *bump*.

"What the hell was that?"

Bump. There it was again. *Bump*. It was coming from my mother's room. I took the stairs two at a time. When I got to the top of the staircase, there it was again. *Bump*.

I got to the doorway of my mother's room and there I saw him. Sylvester had my mother's head gripped firmly in his hands, banging her skull against the wall. *BUMP. BUMP. BUMP. BUMP. BUMP. BUMP.*

Each impact reverberated throughout the room. *BUMP.* The plaster on the wall had cracked. *BUMP.* The wallboard was dented in the shape of my mother's cranium. *BUMP.* A ceramic statue fell to the floor and shattered. It was the image of a small child, exaggerated eyes wide and innocent, arms extended. The caption underneath read, I LOVE YOU THIS MUCH. I had given it to Mom last Mother's Day. I suffered through my allergies for a week, mowing lawns for a dollar a job in order to buy it. *BUMP*. All of my hard work lying in shards on the floor. *BUMP*.

My mother was in her bathrobe, her face streaked with mascara. They hadn't seen me. I had to do something, but what? *BUMP*.

I ran back downstairs into the kitchen. What to do? What to do? No time to start boiling water. What to do? Then, I saw it, there in the sink. The shiny blade of Grandma's butcher knife, its brown handle pointed in my direction. It was the sharpest knife in the house.

Remember that when you were a kid? There was always "the sharpest knife in the house."

"Don't touch that," your mother would admonish. "It's the sharpest knife in the house."

It was as though the knife would cut you just by looking at it.

I grabbed it by its brown handle and took it upstairs. The bumping had stopped. Now Sylvester had her pinned to the wall by her throat. She was choking.

I stood in the doorway, the blade of the knife pointed in his direction. The rage in my gut spewed from my lips. I regurgitated a lifetime of bile. My system was finally throwing up the poison contaminating my young soul.

"Let her go!"

He ignored me.

"Let her go, you son of a bitch."

Sylvester whipped around to face me, his ebony vise still clinched around my mother's windpipe.

"Get the fuck out of here before I whip your ass," he said.

"Let her go or I swear to God I will stick this knife in your fucking heart!"

By the way, I didn't know who this was talking. It sure as hell wasn't me.

"Let her go," I screamed.

The monster was amused. He actually smiled.

"What? You a man now, motherfucker?"

I paused for a moment. The answer was obvious.

"Yes. I'm the man of the house, and I want you to get out!"

My face was wet. Tears.

"Let her go!"

He loosened his grip. She coughed and began to catch her breath.

"Do you know I will kill you?" His stare was cold, steely. It had struck terror in my heart for as long as I could remember. That day, for some reason, it didn't. Like a Jewish boy at his bar mitzvah, that day I was a man.

"Do you know I will kill you?" he repeated.

"You're going to have to if you don't let my mother go."

He looked at me. It was a strange look of—I don't know, admiration? He let her go. He turned . . . and walked toward me.

Oh shit. Now what do I do. I was a little over four feet tall. He was a chiseled mountain of obsidian, a strapping creature sculpted from coal, powerful enough to snap me in two without so much as breaking a sweat. I felt like Admiral Yamamoto after the Pearl Harbor attack. I had awakened the sleeping giant.

He advanced toward me, his eyes ablaze with fury. How dare I be insolent with him? How dare I challenge his warped sense of authority, of demented masculine privilege? I had an inkling of what those black men living under Jim Crow felt as they were dragged from their beds in the dead of night to be punished for some perceived impertinence, "disciplined" for speaking or behaving out of their place. Taught a brutal lesson for being "uppity."

I gripped the knife so tightly that my fingers were numb. I hoped I didn't have to do this. I didn't even know how. Grandma still cut my meat, for God's sake.

Like lightning, he reached for the knife. I slashed blindly at his torso, barely missing his brawny flesh.

"You little motherfucker," he grunted through clenched teeth.

I knew that if I let him catch me, I truly *was* dead. We danced around the room in a death tango. After what seemed like an eternity, he reached for me again. He lunged. Again I struck. This time I hit pay dirt, nicking the outer palm of his right hand. A thick, crimson stream trailed down his arm as he examined the wound. What do you know? The bastard was only human after all.

"Goddammit!" he said as he lunged for me yet again. This time, he grabbed my right wrist. I couldn't move it. I couldn't maneuver the knife. I couldn't defend myself. He had me. He had me and I was going to die. No, dammit! Not like this. Not today.

I balled my left hand into a fist and with all of the force my sixty-pound body could muster, I hit him squarely in the balls. He yelped. It was the sound that a dog makes in the street at the exact moment of impact, the exact moment that the car hits him.

His grip on my wrist loosened, but I still wasn't free. I still couldn't move the knife. I tightened my left again and let loose with the hardest adrenaline-fueled punch I had ever thrown. Again it found its mark. Sylvester's hands dropped to his crotch. His eyes watered and he made a guttural sound. It was his pain that he was trying to mute, now. Welcome to my world, you cocksucker.

I was free. I used the opportunity to back away from him. My wrist hurt, but I was still holding the butcher knife. I still had it.

Now it was Sylvester's turn to catch his breath. He reached for me with both hands. I was watching him every second but I never saw him coming. Before I knew it, he had his hands around my throat. We had been here before. Not again. Please, Lord, not again.

My mother screamed. Her screech was broken by a pounding at the front door.

"Police! Everything all right up there?"

I guess that one of the neighbors must have noticed something "amiss."

I somehow found the air to yell back.

"Help!"

With that, Sylvester took his hands from around my neck. I gasped for air. My neck was bloody. His blood. The next few minutes were a blur. There was the sound of the splinter of wood, footsteps on the staircase, and the crackle of walkie-talkies. Sylvester shook his head in disgust. *He* was disgusted! He pushed past me and walked out the door into the hallway. I could hear him talking to the police as I closed the bedroom door.

I walked over to my mother, who pried the butcher knife from my hand, laid it down on the bed, and hugged me.

"You know," she said, tears streaming down her cheeks and sliding into the nape of her neck, which was turning the plum color of a bruise, "you really shouldn't talk to your father that way."

For the life of me, I never understood what she saw in him. Grandma's husband, Stacy Arbee, her father, my grandfather, was the same guy. He was the same vanishing act, always making promises and then "Poof!" disappearing for years at a time, leaving behind a web of deceit and familial neglect. He was the same guy, the same lazy, sorry, no-good, not-worth-a-damn individual. He was the same man that no one ever accused of not being "a genuine black man." Despite all of that, my mother loved her father—and she loved Sylvester.

My mother was an only child. I've read that only children have difficulties finding and maintaining healthy relationships. Looking at it from an adult perspective, I think that her relationship with Sylvester may have been a reflection of how she saw herself on some level. Though I wasn't an only child, I would have many of the same problems in my own relationships after I grew up. My friends used to tell me that I had a "Henry Higgins complex." I'd find these poor, downtrodden women and try to turn them into "my fair lady."

"So, you live in the gutter? And you're addicted to crystal meth? Repeat after me, 'The rain in Spain . . .' I think I'm in love. I'm gonna date her!"

I worked my way past that, thank God. My mother didn't live long enough to.

CHAPTER 26

Responsibilities

"I first started in real estate in San Leandro. I was called by a party who wished to see a home that was in San Leandro. It was listed by another broker and I requested to show the party the home. I made an appointment, and it was a black family. Before I got back to my office, my broker knew about it from the listing broker, and I was told, I was certainly new in the business and I should wise up."

—Rex Hayes, Hayward, California, Realtor, November, 1971

It was late as I dragged myself down the street toward the apartment complex. I had stayed after school to help Mrs. Carrion grade math quizzes. I loved her. She took me to Foster's Freeze for a root beer float when we were done. If there is anything better than root beer, it's root beer with ice cream. She offered me a ride home but I felt like walking. I had some stuff to think about.

The trial was just a day away and it was bothering me. I was having shortness of breath. My stomach hurt frequently and I was getting dizzy spells. I'd also been having bad dreams. I dreamt I was in court and I said the wrong thing and was dragged off to jail. I didn't want to tell Mom about it. I didn't want her to worry about me. I was the man of the house. My butcher knife escapade had solidified that position once and for all.

As I rounded the corner a half mile from home I heard the familiar drawl.

"Hey theah!"

I looked over to see Mr. Wilkins mowing his lawn. He was wearing his "uniform," as always: Clean white shirt and dirty blue overalls. Did he ever wash those things?

"Hey, Mr. Wilkins," I shouted.

"Come on over here and get some candy."

He always did that to us. Yelled for us to come and get some candy. He never asked us if we wanted any candy. My sisters and I were simply ordered to come and get some candy. He always had Brach's hard candies. Brachs. I didn't really like them. They were like sugar-coated stones.

"I say, come on and git some candy," he shouted again.

"Sure, Mr. Wilkins. Thank you."

Why fight him?

I ambled across the street as he pulled a white handkerchief from his pocket and mopped his sweaty brow. The man was always working. A lot of it was hard physical work: digging, carting wheelbarrows, shoveling. What was he, seventy? Eighty?

"Come on in the workshop while I go get it," he said, turning toward the house.

I followed him into the workshop. It was clean today. He had swept up the sawdust. I noticed these things now because I had become a regular visitor. Tracie and Delisa frequented his place, too. We couldn't walk by the house without being beckoned by him. He was gruff and pushy, but he was a nice man. I'd grown to like him. So had the girls.

A moment later, he emerged from the house with a clenched fist.

"Hold out your hands," he commanded.

I complied and he dropped the little boulders into my palms. I stuffed them into my pockets. They'd be in the apartment complex's Dumpster within the hour.

"Ain't you gonna have none?"

"It's pretty close to dinner. I'll save them for dessert."

I was getting to be a better liar. Survival skills.

"Your grandmamma still using the cutting board I sent her?"

"Yep. She uses it all the time. She cut a roast into steaks on it last night."

That part was true. Grandma loved the cutting board. She brought Mr. Wilkins some of her home-baked rolls in appreciation. Whenever she needed something fixed that was made of wood, she brought it down the street to his house. He cheerfully made the repairs and refused to accept a penny for his work.

"I enjoy it," he always said. "It gives me something to do."

It's so strange. Here we had all of these people being so mean to us, the kids, the Wentworths, the police, even the nuns at school—yet this old white man from Tennessee couldn't do enough nice things for us. Go figure.

"I got something for you to take home," he said.

"You don't have to do that, Mr. Wilkins."

"Hush now. It ain't for you; it's for your grandmamma."

He opened a drawer on his workbench and pulled out a tubular-shaped wad of tissue paper. He unwrapped the paper to reveal a smoothly sanded rolling pin.

"You know what this is?" he asked.

"Yeah. It's one of those things that the wives in cartoons are always hitting their husbands in the head with. I don't think Grandma can use it. She doesn't have a husband."

He chuckled at first; soon the chuckle evolved into a hearty, husky laugh.

"It's a rolling pin. I know your grandmamma bakes. She can use this to roll out her dough."

"Did you make this?"

"Of course," he smiled.

The man was amazing.

"I got those slides back. Sit down and I'll show 'em to you."

One of his many talents was photography. At least once a week he corralled the girls and me on the walk to or from school and made us pose while he snapped a roll of film. He was pretty good. The shots came out well. He never got pictures done though. Only slides.

I sat on a stool at his workbench as he went to one of the wooden desks he had made and opened a drawer. He sorted through several small, yellow Kodak boxes before selecting the one he was looking for. He pulled a stool alongside mine and placed the box in front of me. Written on the box in a shaky blue-inked scrawl were the words, NEGRO CHILDREN — 1975.

Mr. Wilkins removed a small viewer from his coverall pocket, opened the box, removed a slide, and inserted it.

"Look at this," he said proudly.

I peered through the viewer to see Tracie, Delisa, and myself, dressed neatly in our St. Felicitas uniforms (blue cords, white cotton shirt, and bright red sweater for me; the same red sweater with white blouses and ugly plaid, Catholic school skirts for the girls). We were arm in arm. Delisa was laughing and I was smiling. Tracie was showing teeth, but I wouldn't really call her expression a smile. It looked more like she had something crawling up her leg.

"This is very nice, Mr. Wilkins."

He smiled.

"Heah, look at some more."

One at a time, he cycled a dozen more slides through the

viewer. They were all variations on the first shot. As the slides progressed, Tracie loosened up. By the time I got to the last one, she actually looked like she was enjoying herself.

"You know," he said, "if your mama or grandmamma want any of these, I can get some pictures made."

"That would be nice. I'll ask them," I said as he put the slides back into the box and replaced the lid.

I studied the inscription again. NEGRO CHILDREN — 1975.

Mr. Wilkins notice my intense interest.

"What's the matter?"

"Um . . ." I paused.

"What?" he barked.

"My mom says we're not negroes anymore. We're black."

He looked wounded. I had hurt his feelings.

"I'm sorry, Mr. Wilkins. It's no big deal."

"No," he said, pulling a ballpoint pen from a pocket in his overalls. My God, does he have everything in there? "Folks should be called whatever it is they want to be called."

He scratched out the word "negro" and replaced it with "black."

"How's that?" he said, holding the box up for my approval.

I smiled. The smile faded as I thought about something.

"What now?" he said.

"Mr. Wilkins . . . what did you call black people when you were in Tennessee?"

He cast his eyes downward and didn't speak for a long time.

"Tennessee is a different place," he said. His tone was apologetic. "When I lived there it was a different time."

"Oh," I said, sorry that I brought it up.

"Not that it makes things that was wrong, right. It being a different time, I mean."

He got up and put the box of slides back in the drawer.

"Sometimes," he said, fiddling with the contents of the drawer, avoiding eye contact with me, "sometimes when you get older, you notice that things you thought was okay, things you thought was 'just the way it's supposed to be,' ain't okay. It ain't how they supposed to be at all."

"Do people ever change?" I asked.

"Some people do. Others . . ." He shook his head. "Some folks are too 'right' to realize they wrong."

"Were you ever wrong, Mr. Wilkins?"

He shut the drawer. His gaze still avoided mine.

"Let's just say there are things that I would change if I could. Things I might've done different." He finally looked at me. "We all got to take some kind of responsibility," he said.

He pulled a handkerchief from his pocket and mopped his brow.

"But, there's no sense in talkin' about that now. What's done is done. Alls you can do is what you can do today. You can't ever do nothing about yesterday."

I nodded.

"How's your mama's court case?"

"You know about that?"

"Your grandmamma told me. It's soon, ain't it?"

I nodded again.

"Tomorrow. I have to testify."

"You okay 'bout that?"

I paused. My turn to avoid eye contact now.

"I just don't want to say the wrong thing."

He nodded.

"I think I should go. It's getting late," I said,

I got up and walked toward the door of the workshop, Mr. Wilkins at my side. As I opened the door, he put his hand on my shoulder.

"I think it's a brave thing your mama's doing."

"Yeah."

"Wait a minute," he said. "You forgot the rolling pin."

He walked back to the workbench, rewrapped the pin in the paper, and handed it to me.

"I don't want to hear you been hitting your sisters in the head with this," he smiled.

I smiled back.

"You'll be okay. In court I mean. Folks got to speak up when things ain't right. I know that there are times I wish that I'd . . ." His voice trailed off. "You head on home. I'll see ya. Don't forget to ask your people if they want me to get some pictures made from the slides."

I nodded as I walked out the door and headed toward home. As I walked, I tried to picture Mr. Wilkins as a young man. Was he good with wood then? Did he take pictures? Would he have been nice to me? Or would he have been one of those folks driving by yelling, "nigger"? Then, I stopped myself. I remembered what he said about yesterday. Nothing can be done. You have to think about today.

I always wondered about Mr. Wilkins. I wondered what was in his past. Had he been a part of the white mobs I'd seen in old Civil Rights–era footage? Had he done something he wasn't proud of? Or worse yet, seen something he could have stopped but didn't? Were all of those rolling pins, pictures, and hard candies some kind of atonement for the things from yesterday that he couldn't (or didn't) do anything about?

"*We all got to take some kind of responsibility,*" he had said. Responsibility for what?

I'd never find out. Not too long after the trial, he was gone. He just disappeared. Word in the neighborhood was that he had some family members who thought he was too old to take care of himself. That was, at least in my opinion, ridiculous. Every time I ever saw the man, he was performing some type of labor. It was always hard physical labor: digging, hauling dirt in his wheelbarrow, sawing, hammering, sanding, and painting. To say that this man with the constitution of a bull was somehow unable to care for himself was laughable. I can't do most of the things he did now, and I'm probably less than half the age he was at that time. Regardless, his family apparently moved him back to Tennessee. I never saw Josiah Wilkins again.

I had lied to Mr. Wilkins. I didn't really have to rush home. In fact, I was in no real hurry to get home. I just didn't want to talk about the trial. I didn't even want to think about it. I knew that once I got home, Grandma would have me laying out my suit and polishing my shoes. Mom would be telling me for the umpteenth time what to expect when we got into court. I didn't want to do this, but I had responsibilities. The man of the house. I had fought for the title and I had to take what came with it.

Because I was still not ready to go home I took a short detour to Jon's house. I had been meaning to talk to him anyway. The last couple of days he'd seemed down. Once he even looked like he'd been crying. I didn't know what the problem was, but I could certainly understand his wanting to keep it to himself. I hadn't told him about the trial. Not a word. Not about the lawsuit or the Wentworths or the busted sewer pipe or anything.

As I approached Jon's big yellow tract house, I realized that I'd walked right past the "cop spot" and I hadn't given it a second thought. I guess I went to Jon's house so often, and I walked that path so frequently, that it didn't bother me anymore. Jon had been more of a friend than he even knew.

Jon stood in his front yard, his eyes cast downward as he forced a manual lawnmower over a clump of crabgrass. Despite my allergies and the fact that I didn't have a yard, I had gotten pretty good with gardening tools. Jon and I sometimes took his mom's stuff and went from house to house offering to cut his neighbors' grass. We would cut the grass, pull the weeds, and clip the hedges, then we'd bag and haul away the yard trimmings—all for a dollar. If they wanted both the front and the back yards done, we charged two dollars. It was hard work, but it kept us in comic book money.

Jon didn't see me as he pushed the mower over the crab-grass, watched it get stuck, backed it up, and then pushed it again—only to watch it stick in the same place. He repeated this procedure three or four times, his face getting redder each time. Suddenly he threw the mower to the ground and started to cry.

"Hey," I said.

He wiped his eyes and noticed me for the first time.

"Hey," he said.

"The blades probably need sharpening. I noticed it when we cut the lawn next door the other day."

"Yeah," he said, still wiping at his eyes.

"Where do you get that done? Are there guys who do that?"

"Do what?"

"Sharpen lawnmower blades."

"I think so. I'll have to ask my mom."

"You know what we should do, Jon? We should save up and get a power mower. It would make it a lot faster to cut grass and we could do a lot more lawns. What do you think?"

"That's a good idea," he said, barely composed.

"We should find out how much they cost."

"They have them at Gemco," he said. "We can go look if you want."

"Yeah," I said after a brief pause. I hadn't told him about that incident either. Maybe it would be different if he was with me. "You want to go Saturday?"

He put his left arm over his eyes and began to sob.

"It doesn't have to be Saturday. Sunday's okay, too. After I get back from mass," I blurted out, not knowing what else to say. I have never been good with sadness, not my own and certainly not other people's.

"My parents are getting a divorce."

"Oh. Wow." Now my eyes cast downward to the patch of crabgrass.

I had seen Jon's dad on quite a few occasions up to that time. He was (and is) a nice guy. He played basketball with us and took us for ice cream sometimes. I never really thought about how he didn't live at Jon's house. It suddenly occured to me that he hadn't been at Jon's birthday party. Funny, it didn't seem odd to me, then. Sylvester had never been around on any of my birthdays. I was so used to what the rest of the world would consider abnormal that it seemed perfectly normal to me.

"Are you sure?" I asked him.

He nodded, crying harder.

I walked over and I hugged him. I had never hugged another boy before. I had hugged my sisters when they fell down and scraped a knee or when they cried because they had broken one of their toys, but this was different. Still, it felt natural. My brother was in pain and I hugged him.

"I know how you feel. My parents are divorced, too."

I knew that this wasn't exactly true, but it wasn't that far off the mark. As far as I was concerned, they might as well have been divorced. I *wanted* them to be divorced. Jon's situation was different. As far as I knew, he never had to fend off his dad with a butcher knife. Every time I ever saw his dad touch him, it was with kindness. The sort of subtle contact; a pat on the back, using an index finger to push his blond hair out of his eyes, fingertips laid gently upon Jon's cheek, all gestures saying, "I love you." I envied Jon a little bit for that. When I thought of Sylvester's touch, I thought of how rough the skin on his palms felt when his hands were clamped around my throat.

"Hey, your dad will still be around, right?"

Jon sniffed.

"That's what he said. But he won't live with us."

I nodded. He was the man of the house now, too.

Once again, he had shown me that I wasn't the only one. I guess every family has its stuff.

Mom always said, "We all have our crosses to bear."

Perspective is a funny thing. As with most issues, Jon helped me find mine.

"I better get back to this," Jon said. "Mom wants it done by the time she gets home from work."

He wiped his eyes with his arm again. They were red, but dry.

I walked over and picked up the mower. I positioned it in front of the patch of crabgrass and placed both of my hands on the right side of the handle. Jon looked at me, then at the mower. He grabbed the left side. Together we pushed and pulled until the patch was a memory. As I wiped the sweat from my forehead, Jon smiled.

CHAPTER 27

Judgment Day

"You say, sir, that you have concerns about creating a ghetto. I would submit to you that you already have a ghetto. An all-white ghetto. The reason for the fear and the prejudice in that community is because of their isolation. Perhaps it's time for the community to do something about the racial prejudice, because this is a racists' community. And it's right on the bridge of Oakland. And it's bound to spill over and have some harmful effects unless the community will decide to do something about it."

—Commissioner F.M. Freeman
U.S. Commission on Civil Rights hearings, May 6, 1967

September 10, 1975. Judgment Day. Mom and Grandma had testified yesterday. Today, it was my turn.

What Mr. Ware was trying to prove was a constant and deliberate pattern of harassment of my mother by the defendants. My mother had begun seeing a psychiatrist the previous summer. Mr. Ware had him evaluate her for emotional distress. He testified. My mother's best friend and coworker, Sherry Moniz, had heard some of the harassing phone calls that Starr and his people had made to their place of employment. She testified.

Mrs. Pat Imburgia also bravely stepped up to the plate for us. Mrs. Imburgia was a white lady who lived in our building.

She had the same number of family members that we did, yet she was not harassed, threatened, or evicted on the basis of it. That changed when this courageous single mother agreed to testify on my mother's behalf. It was made known to her by the apartment management that to participate "would not be in the best interest of her family." She ignored the intimidation and testified anyway.

I was to testify that Mr. Wentworth had illegally entered our apartment, thus making my mother feel insecure in the privacy of her own home. Proving emotional distress would mean . . . money. I like money. Money is a good thing. But there's also justice. Starr was a multimillionaire. You can't put rich people in jail for calling you a nigger. The way that you hurt them is by taking their money.

I waited in the witness room. I was nervous but prepared. I had been watching *Perry Mason* reruns religiously for weeks. I figured that if I was going to be a lawyer, my education might as well start there. What better teacher than a lawyer who never lost a case?

Most important, Grandma had taken me to get a haircut the day before, as well as a new pair of dress shoes. My head and my feet looked okay. How could we lose?

Soon, Mr. Ware came to get me.

"You ready?" he asked.

"Uh-huh."

"Okay, don't be nervous, son. Just tell the truth."

"Just tell the truth," I repeated as I nodded and patted my neatly trimmed afro.

"Just tell the truth," I repeated.

Looking back over the span of all these years, I have to smile at the irony of Mr. Ware telling *me* to "just tell the truth."

I walked into the courtroom and I was amazed. It had looked so much bigger on *Perry Mason*. There was a bailiff and a court reporter, attorneys for both sides, Starr, the Wentworths, and Mom. There was no jury. The case would be decided by the judge. The white judge.

"Raise your right hand and repeat after me," the bailiff instructed gruffly. "Do you swear to tell the truth, the whole truth, and nothing but the truth, so help you God?"

I always wondered, what do atheists do at a time like this?

Yeah, I swear, God, Santa Claus, the Easter Bunny. So help me Rhonda. Help, help me Rhonda.

"I swear," I timidly answered the bailiff.

He grunted a soft, "Be seated."

I sat, as Mr. Ware fired a barrage of questions at me.

"Were you home alone?"

"Did someone enter the apartment?"

"Who was it?"

"And what did Mr. Wentworth say when you caught him?"

"Your witness."

The other attorney got up. He was a big, red-faced, constipated-looking guy.

"Brian," he growled. "Brian, do you think that your mother wants you to lie here today?"

Immediately I was on my feet.

"Objection, your honor," I shouted, taking everyone by surprise. Out of the corner of my eye, I could see the judge trying to suppress a smile. I went through a litany of all of the objections I'd heard Perry Mason and Hamilton Burger make.

"Counsel is on a fishing expedition," I said. "It's improper cross-examination, no proper foundation was laid for that question. It's incompetent, irrelevant, immaterial, and it calls for a conclusion on the part of the witness."

I thought that was damned good, myself.

"Your honor," Mr. Constipation bellowed.

The judge said, "Don't look at me. He's right!"

Yes. Yes, all that *Perry Mason* viewing paid off!

"Fine," the attorney acquiesced. "I'll withdraw the question."

At least, that's how I like to remember it. Imagination is a wonderful gift.

I had him on the run, or at least I thought so. Until he asked the next question.

"Brian, have you ever seen your mother and father fight?"

The words were a blow to the gut that sent the air from my body. I couldn't speak. What was he asking me this question for?

What I didn't know at the time was that the defendants had obtained a copy of the police report from the day I'd pulled the knife on Sylvester. They were trying to undercut my mother's claim of emotional distress by saying that any distress she suffered in her life was a direct result of her marriage. All I knew was that I was a little boy and I was being asked to talk about family business *outside the family*. And that's not a black thing to do. What do I do?

"Have you ever seen your parents fight?" he shouted at me.

I looked at my mom and her eyes seemed to say, "It's okay," as she slowly nodded her head.

"Yes," I answered in a barely audible voice.

"And have you ever seen your father hurt your mother?"

I fought hard but I was losing. I couldn't hold them back. The tears were winning as they streamed down my cheeks. I looked at my lap.

"Yes," I whispered.

I finished testifying and I felt sick. I went back to the witness room and had some root beer. A little while later, I heard the courtroom door open and I came outside where I found my mother seated on one of the wooden benches. She was surrounded by Grandma, Sherry Moniz, and Mr. Ware, and she was crying.

"I just hope that the judge gives us enough time to find a place to live."

CHAPTER 28

Get Your Black Ass Up!

999. I sat like a blob on the couch in my living room. I didn't know how long I had been there in that position. A day? A week? It was all a haze. I wanted to go outside and play Twister with my kids. I wanted to laugh and contort my body from left foot red to right hand blue, but I just didn't have it in me. It was like gravity was holding me down. I was a damaged mind trapped inside a useless, nonfunctioning body. The familiar stasis of my childhood molasses held me firmly in its grip.

The tears came. I wanted to go outside, but I couldn't get up. I couldn't get up, dammit. I couldn't get up.

The phone next to me rang. I ignored it. It rang for a while longer and then stopped. I buried my wet face in my hands as the ringing began anew. Again, I let it go unanswered until it stopped. A few more moments passed, the only noise in the room my ever-increasing wail. It rang again. This time I picked it up.

"Hello," I managed to get out.

"Brian," the familiar voice said. "It's Grandma."

I didn't say anything as I sniffled into the receiver. Why the hell had I answered the phone?

"Boy," she finally asked, "what's wrong with you?"

All pretense of composure vanished with that question.

"Grandma," I sobbed. "They finally got me. I lost control and they won."

A beat. Was she still there?

"Grandma," I said, crying so hard that my voice took on a husky hoarseness, "Grandma, I can't get up."

More silence.

"You can't get up?" she finally said in that incredulous way of speaking that Grandma has. That tone that seems to say, "Quit playing and do what I told your ass to do." "What you mean you can't get up?" she said.

Suddenly, her voice changed. It was firmer, harsher. Enraged.

"Boy, you better not *never* say you can't get up! *Never*, do you hear me? Don't you think there was times I didn't want to get up? When your mother passed and left me alone with all of y'all all by myself, what if I would have said that? Or when your grandfather left me alone with a newborn while he was off running in the street somewhere? What if I would've said that? I been hungry, I been broke, I been cold, and I been alone, but I still did what I had to do when I had to do it."

I was sniffling harder now. I didn't need this. Then again, maybe I did.

"You can't get up," she said, mocking me. "Boy, you ought to be shamed. I'm shamed of you. GET YOUR ASS UP! GET YOU BLACK ASS UP NOW!!"

I was stunned; shocked by her words. Where the hell was the sympathy? Where was the empathy? Where was the compassion? I was in pain. I was in horrible, terrible, unbearable, and excruciating pain. Where was the maternal comfort, love, and support I needed from the woman who had raised me? Where? Where was it?

Then it hit me in the face like a cold blast of winter wind. Grandma, the child of Jim Crow, the granddaughter of slaves.

Grandma, who always played whatever hand she was dealt no matter what. Grandma, who always stood her ground no matter how hard people tried to knock her off of it. Grandma.

There was something about the sound of her voice that could cut through drama and self-importance like a hot knife through a cold stick of butter. She was the voice of reason, the voice of my past, my present, and, I realized for the first time, my future. She was the reason that I got here in the first place and the reason I'd made it on this earth as long as I had.

She didn't say anything else. She didn't need to. I hung up the phone, I put my feet on the floor, and I got up. Then I went outside and I played Twister with my kids. And I laughed. For the first time in memory, I laughed a deep, hearty, infectious, and healing laugh. At that moment I was overcome with an incredible sense of identity. I felt . . . black.

CHAPTER 29

End Game

"These are just two of the tens of thousands of reasons that blacks are not welcome in my neighborhood."

> —Anonymous letter sent to the author by a San Leandro resident in 2004. The envelope contained two newspaper clippings involving violent crime. In one of the clippings, the criminal suspect was white.

R ecently, I was able to get hold of some of the surviving court records from the trial. It turns out that the judge ruled that Mr. Wentworth *never entered our apartment that day.* He didn't believe me. It never occurred to me that he wouldn't believe me, because I was telling the truth. Kids always think that people will believe the truth. As adults, we learn differently, don't we?

It turns out that he didn't believe my mother either. He ruled that any emotional distress she suffered was the direct result of her marriage to my father. The finding of fact called her "delusional" and "prone to fantasy." So much for justice. Apparently this means that you can do anything to the poor, anything to the abused and the downtrodden, because their pain and suffering, their misery, is the result of their own unfortunate circumstances. No amount of harassment or degradation has any merit because it pales in comparison to their already-sorry state of affairs. My mother got no money.

Our apartment, that Friday night.

"It's my deal!" Tracie shouted.

"No, it's my . . . okay. Go ahead, you can deal," I surrendered.

My mother smiled. Things hadn't turned out quite as badly as she'd thought. The judge also ruled that the eviction was unwarranted. We didn't have to move.

"Gee, I don't have anything," Mom said, looking at her cards. Then she suddenly slapped a joker to her forehead. "Except this."

A little more than three years later, my mother would finally run out of jokers.

"Gal, you got another wild card?" Grandma spat. "Shit!"

Grandma would live in that apartment for another twenty-three years, until Tracie and I bought her a house. She's eighty-five now and she stays busy running behind her thirteen great-grandchildren.

"Look, Mommy," Tracie said, slapping a joker to her forehead. "I don't got no wild cards. See?"

"Double negative. Very good!" Mom smiled.

Tracie would stop sucking her thumb, lose her lisp, and become a successful model, businesswoman, wife, and mother. I'm very proud of her. My other sisters would follow suit and fulfill my mother's middle-class dreams.

As for Sylvester, he never came back after I threw him out of the house that day. As far as I know, my mother never saw him again.

Things got better after the trial. Starr eventually sold the apartment complex as more and more blacks moved in. The Wentworths were replaced by other managers who didn't harass us. Best of all, I met some of the really wonderful people who made it possible for me to grow up in San Leandro.

People like Joe Zipp and Mike Trutner, my scoutmasters.

People like Marylou Ramirez, my eighth-grade teacher, who nurtured me, put me on the stage for the first time, and told me that I was worth something. Jon Regan, who befriended me when we were just nine years old and is still my best friend. Skinny, uncoordinated Jon would grow into an incredible high school athlete and, later, to my shock and amazement, into a United States Marine. The little boy who couldn't get a push mower over a clump of crabgrass graduated boot camp near the top of his class, earning the distinction of marksman and a promotion to corporal. Who would have thought? He's married to a wonderful woman and has three kids. I'm the proud godfather to his oldest son, Joshua.

There's our dear family friend Charlene Raimondi who's been looking after me since I was ten. Unbeknownst to me until recently, she paid for my mother's coffin so that Mom wouldn't be buried in what was literally a wooden box. Charlene still looks after me to this very day.

There was Tommy Thomas, my CYO baseball coach when I was ten, who later opened the first comedy club in San Leandro, Tommy T's Comedy House. He gave me my start in showbusiness at eighteen. He encouraged me and hired me to perform even in the beginning when I wasn't very good, and gave me the opportunity to discover that my true calling wasn't civil rights law after all. His kindness and confidence in me gave me the ability to find my professional path. For that, I will always be grateful.

My fifth-grade teacher, Lisa Carrion, and her father, Mr. Duchard, did a kind and amazing thing. Lisa and my mother connected on a level, the depth of which I still don't fully understand. What I later found out was that after Mom died, Lisa and her dad secretly paid my Catholic high school tuition. They never said a word to me. They just wrote checks.

And then, there was Paul Cromwell, the father of one of my St. Felicitas classmates. Dear, sweet, kind Mr. Cromwell. I found out at his funeral that his own family never knew that after Mom died, he came over every Christmas Eve and brought Grandma money to make sure that we had things for Christmas.

These are the people who changed San Leandro, and they're the reason that I still live here today. According to the 2000 census, today San Leandro is one of the most diverse cities in the state of California. Take that, San Francisco!

If you walk down the streets of San Leandro today, you'll see people of all races, creeds, and colors. They go to work together. They sit next to each other in school and shop together in the same stores. Some of the old attitudes persist. There remains an ignorant minority, primarily some members of the older population, who long for the "good old days." (Have you ever noticed how black folks are never part of "the good old days," or "simpler times"?) This small faction is dying off, though. A good friend of mine, a successful businessman and entrepreneur in San Leandro, put it best when he said that the racial attitudes of San Leandro have changed "coffin by coffin."

I have a friend who has been a member of the San Leandro Police Department since the 1980s. At the time that my friend, a native of Chicago, joined the force, he was one of the few African-American officers in the department. He took the job here with no knowledge of the city's history. He recently related to me the story of one of his first police calls.

Responding to a 911 call, my friend arrived at a San Leandro home and knocked on the door. An elderly white woman answered. She took one look at this black man in a policeman's uniform standing on her front porch and said, "I'm sorry. I didn't call the Oakland Police Department. I wanted San Leandro's."

Old stereotypes die hard. So hard, in fact, that it is difficult for some people to believe I still live here among all these ghosts. Upon thoughtful reflection, I would have to say that it is, at least in part, due to the strength and resilience of my mother. She fought too long and too hard for us to be here for me not to take advantage of all of the opportunities that this community has to offer. It seemed to me, as a young man just out of high school, that to bolt the first chance I got would almost be disrespectful. If I left, what was her fight for? She was no longer alive to stand her ground. I was determined to stand it for her.

The aforementioned friends and benefactors are the second major factor that keeps me in San Leandro. The third is that even though things have gotten better in immeasurable ways, there is still some work to do.

In recent months, several of the Bay Area's newspapers and electronic media outlets have run features on my family's story and my mother's fight, as well as what I'd discovered about the institutionalized racism that existed in the city's real estate industry. Several journalists reported to me that they received calls and nasty letters (anonymous of course) from some of the older San Leandro residents, livid about the exposure and angry about my "dredging up the past."

A columnist from one of the major dailies told me about the woman who called his office to complain about the complimentary article he'd written about my work.

"Why couldn't he and his family have just lived where the black people lived?" she demanded to know.

Without missing a beat the writer said, "Ma'am, may I please have your name and phone number so that I can call you when I do an article on bigots?"

Not surprising, she hung up.

Then there was the woman who apparently listened to every radio and television interview I gave on the subject. I say "apparently" because, following my appearances, the show's producers and/or hosts would immediately receive an e-mail tirade on how I was making the whole thing up and how she had lived in this town since the 1940s and there had never been any prejudice or racism in the city of San Leandro.

Part of her rationale is that the city has always been "a melting pot," which she would illustrate by rattling off all of the white European countries represented in town.

I e-mailed the woman myself, gave her my sources, and invited her to look them up. She of course said, "I don't need to look them up!"

"Coffin by coffin."

There has been some "white flight" from my generation as well. Many of the kids I grew up with, whose parents fled to San Leandro to avoid the growing ethnic diversity of Oakland, now reside in the bedroom communities of nearby Southern Alameda and Contra Costa counties. Suburbs like Alamo, Danville, San Ramon, Walnut Creek, Orinda, and Dublin are the new San Leandros. They boast mainly white communities made up of folks who want to live by people who look and think as they do.

A few years back, when the movie *Malcolm* X opened at a San Ramon multiplex, it was widely reported that someone changed the marquee to read MALCOLM NIGGER.

I recently ran into a man I'd gone to grade school with who was telling me he had moved to one of these suburbs. I asked why so many San Leandro residents of our generation were bolting to these areas. His response?

"Too much overflow from Oakland."

The more things change, the more they stay the same.

There are still some problems with housing discrimination

in the area as well, but nothing like in the 1970s. The folks from the local chapter of Fair Housing tell me that, in recent years, they have caught some landlords using a technique they call "vocal profiling." A representative of Fair Housing will call and inquire about a home or apartment for rent speaking in a stereotypical "black dialect." "Ebonics," if you will. Some landlords contacted will say that the unit is no longer available. A few minutes later, the Fair Housing representative calls back using "standard English" and is invited by the landlord to come out and inspect the property.

I think of the fun my mother could have had with this using her British "credit extension" voice.

In April 2004, San Leandro Mayor Sheila Young presented Grandma and, posthumously, my mother, with a city commendation for their bravery in fighting to make San Leandro a more diverse, inclusive community. Although Grandma, my sisters, and their families moved to the Sacramento area in 2001 to take advantage of less expensive housing opportunities, Mayor Young issued a proclamation making Grandma forever an honorary resident of the city of San Leandro.

"This makes me want to move back to San Leandro," Grandma said.

Although I didn't let her know that I'd seen them, she had tears in her eyes. I was more than a little misty myself as I thought about Mom looking down on what she'd set in motion. I could feel her smiling.

I put my own house in order as well. I left the morning show job to focus on what I love—writing and comedy. I continued my medical treatment and obtained the services of a good therapist who has helped me battle the demons I had kept at bay for so long. Unfortunately, the weight of the depression was too much for my marriage to my children's mother, and we divorced. It is often said that when one door closes, another one opens. I guess there's truth to that. After the dust settled, I met and married the love of my life, Susie. All of the good changes in my life enabled me to find the strength and courage to talk about these issues publicly. I did so in the best way that I knew how: on the stage.

I had spent my entire life doing stand-up material on politics and popular culture but I had never done anything personal. I had never really told my audiences the truth. I decided that it was time to cleanse my soul and exorcise my demons once and for all. In order to do that, I knew that I had to be naked up there on the stage (metaphorically speaking, of course) and not hold anything back. Not even the thing I was most embarrassed about in the world—my "gesture."

The play *Not a Genuine Black Man* opened at The Marsh theater in San Francisco in April of 2004. Originally scheduled for a six-week stint, it went on to run for two years—becoming the longest-running solo show in San Francisco history.

During the show's run, I met so many other black men whose lives have mirrored my own. They were the first blacks in the suburbs of Philadelphia, the white enclaves of southern California, the homogenized communities of Wisconsin, Iowa, Idaho, and Minnesota. I met Asian men and women who have been castigated by those who share their race because they're "too white." They're called "bananas" and "Twinkies" because they are "yellow on the outside and white on the inside." I've met elderly women who endured extreme isolation as the first Jews in their midwestern suburban neighborhoods, and Latinos criticized for too readily embracing European culture and values. They are ridiculed as "coconuts," another "white on the inside" metaphor. They, too, thought that they were alone, that they were the only ones of their kind in the universe. That they were not "normal."

I was also surprised to learn that I wasn't alone in fighting depression, either. Many people I've known for years, people who I thought "had it all together," have opened up to me about their battles with the disease. It helped me to understand that depression is indeed an illness and that those afflicted with it should not be any more embarrassed or ashamed about it than they would be if they were diagnosed with cancer or diabetes.

One of the most touching moments I experienced in this regard was after a performance one night when a young professional woman approached me and stoically confided, "I think about killing myself every day. After hearing your story, I'm going to call someone tomorrow and get help."

Wow.

I'm a firm believer that most things in this world happen for a reason. We don't always know whose reason or for what reason, but there is a purpose. It turns out that the difficult period I went through was not purgatory after all. I was indeed saved from the finality of what could have happened in the garage for a reason. To tell the other "Oreos," "coconuts," and "Twinkies" and whatever other pejoratives the race police decide to bestow upon those who don't subscribe to their interpretation of what it means to "keep it real," that they are okay. *They are normal.* We must all live our lives in the way that makes use the most comfortable and the happiest.

Whether it's considered "black" or not, I still love Rick Springfield's music. I open for him every opportunity I get and I never miss one of his new CDs. If there's anybody in the "'hood" who's got a problem with that, tough.

But even after coming to terms with all of these issues and settling them, I realized that I still had one piece of unfinished business.

CHAPTER 30

Pappy

I t was an early spring evening. I like those nights when the clocks have been set ahead an hour and the sun doesn't go down until seven or so. It was my third night parked out there, indiscreetly I thought, just watching the building. It wasn't much. Just an old store front that was now decades past its retail prime, living a new twenty-first-century life as a place for the indigent.

I got a sudden twinge of familiarity. I was on a stakeout again. It had been over twenty years since I last did this. That time was during my sophomore year in college. I got a part-time job as a Pinkerton Investigator, working out of the San Francisco office—the same office the great Dashiell Hammett had worked in while scribbling his potboilers for detective magazines like *Black Mask*. I only lasted the summer as a sleuth, but what I'd learned was coming in handy today. Park on a sidestreet where you can see your target. Make sure you're in a nondescript vehicle. Don't do anything to draw attention to yourself. Be as inconspicuous as possible.

I sat there in the Miata. It was no different from the millions of other Miatas on the road, save for its history as an instrument of attempted suicide. I sat and I read the paper and made cell phone calls. There had been two fruitless nights so far. Maybe this one would be a bust as well. Maybe, even if

I achieved my objective, it would still be a bust. I didn't even know what I was doing there. What the hell did I expect to accomplish? My wife certainly didn't think it was a good idea, so I hadn't told her how I was spending my evenings. Only that I was going out to run some errands. Sitting there alone those evenings, I spent a lot of time in my own head. I mulled over things I hadn't remembered in decades. I remembered Pappy.

When I was a kid, the part of school I dreaded most was Monday morning. The kids would all come in and talk about the neat things they'd done with their fathers over the weekend. We were regaled with tales of fishing trips and 49er games, campouts and model rocket launches. I had no dad stories. I was left out yet again, faced with one more area where I lacked a common frame of reference.

Then, one Friday night, I couldn't sleep so I got up and turned on the television. While flipping the channels, I chanced upon an old black-and-white 1950s TV series starring James Garner. It was a Western called *Maverick. Maverick* was the story of two poker-playing brothers, Bret (played by Garner) and Bart (played by Jack Kelly) who traveled the old west going from card table to card table. They were witty, sophisticated, and smarter than most of the people they met up with, and yet they were cowards who would rather run or fast-talk their way out of a fight than throw a punch. I immediately related to them.

The Maverick brothers had one other characteristic that endeared me to them. Every episode, they found an opportunity to quote their wise father, a man they called "Pappy." The quotes were funny, erudite, and practical in a roguish sort of way. When challenged to a gunfight, Bret might say, "As my old Pappy used to say, a coward dies a thousand deaths, a hero only one. A thousand to one's a pretty good advantage." When being accused of leaving the poker table while he was ahead, Bart might retort, "As my dear Pappy used to say, the only time to quit when you're winning is when you've won it all." You never saw Pappy, but his presence loomed as large on the series as that of the brothers.

The following Monday morning, when one of the boys was going on and on about the barbecue pit he and his father had built over the weekend, I chimed in.

"As my old Pappy used to say, the two biggest evils in life are hard liquor and hard work."

The kids laughed.

When I came to school late one morning and the boys wanted to know where I'd been, I said, "In the words of my old Pappy, time waits for no man . . . unless he has a broken watch."

Again, they laughed.

I finally had a father. Not a father who did stuff with me, but a father who was charming, witty, and wise. Nobody ever asked me where he was or how often I saw him or what he did for a living. Luckily, nobody was staying up past midnight on school nights to catch *Maverick* reruns or the jig would have been up. Pappy became as much a fixture in the schoolyard as the fathers of the other boys. He had sage advice for every occasion. Some I took verbatim from James Garner; other gems of wisdom I wrote myself in a spiral notebook I kept. I was always waiting for just the right opening to unleash the perfect "Pappyism."

I was smiling and thinking about "Pappy" when the screech of tires brought my attention back to the storefront. A man who had crossed the street against the light just missed being roadkill by a matter of seconds.

"Why the fuck don't you watch where you're going?" he yelled in an obvious attempt to save face.

It was the same attitude. The same sense that whatever he wanted to do was what would be done, and the hell with the rest of the world. It was still, "Quit cutting you eyes at me."

Sylvester made his way across the street and went into the place. He looked smaller than I remembered him. It could have been that I was bigger now. It could also have been the colon cancer that I heard was ravaging his body. He was only fifty-nine, but he looked much older. Maybe, with enough of life's abuse, black will indeed crack.

Through contacts I have in law enforcement, I had tracked him to this shelter. It had been twenty-five years since I'd seen him last. A few months before my sixteenth birthday, I had gone looking for him. In spite of all of the pain and the misery he'd caused, despite all of the anguish and hurt he'd brought to my spirit and my soul, he was still my father. My mother was gone and I was a teenager in search of a man's guidance. For better or worse, I needed my Pappy.

I found him working on a loading dock in San Leandro, not far from the apartment complex. Learning this made me angry at first. It had been years since the knife incident, and he knew that Mom was dead because his own mother had attended the funeral. This also meant that he knew that Grandma was raising his children all by herself, and here he was just a few miles away and he never even bothered to look in on us. He never cared enough to see if Grandma needed anything.

I pushed all of that to the back of my mind.

"Water under the bridge," I said to myself as I walked up to him as he hoisted a large box onto a truck.

"You got big," he said when he saw me.

"Yeah. I'll be sixteen soon."

"I've got a break in a couple minutes. Let's get something to eat," he said, taking off his heavy leather gloves.

We went to a local Denny's and talked for a long time. I told him about school and my sisters. I told him my dreams for the future. It was nice. It was the first time I remembered having a conversation with him about anything.

That meal turned into many. I would come by his work and we'd go have hamburgers or eggs and talk.

"Your birthday's next week," he said one night at dinner.

"Yeah. Monday."

"I want to get you something," he said. "Something to make up for a lot of birthdays."

I set the hamburger I was nibbling down on my plate and looked at him with anticipation. He'd never given me anything, ever.

"I have a buddy who has a car dealership in Oakland. On Tuesday, I want you to take off school early, around lunchtime. I'm gonna pick you up and take you there to get a car of your own."

I didn't know what to say.

"Really?" was all I could blurt out.

"Now, it won't be a new car. I can't afford that. But I'm sure we can find something you'll like."

"Thanks, Dad. I don't know what to say."

"Don't say anything. It's something I owe you."

A car! I was going to get my own car!

For the next week, I walked on air. I told my buddies that I'd be tooling around in wheels of my own. I scoured car magazines and used car ads to get some ideas about what I might want to drive. I talked to mechanics I knew about what to look for and what to avoid once we got to the car lot.

The night before my birthday was like Christmas Eve when I was a kid. I was so excited I could barely sleep. I was turning sixteen, and I was going to get my license and my own car. It would be the best birthday ever.

Grandma wrote me a note asking that I be excused from school at ten for a doctor's appointment. She picked me up and took me to the Department of Motor Vehicles to get my driver's license. She had the foresight to realize that I would want to drive my car home from the lot once I got it. That would be half the fun. I aced the test and was home sitting in my living room by noon. Sylvester was to arrive around lunchtime. Grandma made me a birthday lunch that I was too excited to eat.

I sat watching the door like a puppy dog waiting for its master to return from work. Soon it was one o'clock. Then two. Then three. No Sylvester. I wanted to call him and see how late he was running, but I couldn't. I didn't have his home phone number. I didn't even know where he lived. I called his work, but was reminded that his shift didn't start until nine in the evening. Soon it was six o'clock. Then seven. I still sat in the chair looking at the door, forlorn.

"Come on in and have something to eat," Grandma said, putting her hand on my shoulder. "I made your birthday dinner, lasagna, just like you asked me to."

"I'm not hungry, Grandma."

I sat in that living room until Grandma finally insisted that I eat something and get into bed. The next night, I called Sylvester's job. I was told that he was no longer employed there. I never saw or heard from him again. Twenty-five years. Now I sat watching this angry little man jaywalk into a homeless shelter. Now what? Do I go in after him? If I do, what should I say? What do I want to say?

I used to have dreams where he'd walk up to me with his arms stretched wide to hug me.

"Son . . ." he'd say right before I decked him.

"I'm not a little boy anymore and I'm not a woman. Let's see how you fight now, you son of a bitch!"

That feeling wasn't there that evening. I just wanted to ask *why?* Why were you so mean? Why did you hurt us that way? Why didn't you do the things that a father is supposed to do? Why didn't you take me camping and give me an allowance? Why didn't you teach me how to talk to girls? How to throw a curve ball? How to survive as a black man in this society? Why didn't you give me sage advice like Pappy? Why didn't you show up on my birthday? Why? Why?

As I pondered these questions I saw him walk back out of the building. Before I knew it, I was out of the car and walking in his direction. He moved slower than I remembered, his pace laggard with age and disease. I was within five feet of him before I finally said something.

"Excuse me," I said.

He turned and looked me in the face.

"Yeah?"

"Do . . . you know what time it is?"

It was all I could think of to say.

He looked at an old watch on his wrist.

"Quarter to seven."

"Um . . . thanks," I said as I watched him turn and jaywalk back across the street. He didn't know who I was. All of this trouble, all of this anxiety, and he didn't even know who I was.

I walked back to the Miata in a daze and started the motor. I was halfway home when I burst into laughter. It was a side-splitting, hearty laughter that made me lose control of my faculties. I had to pull the car over to the shoulder of the road. I was laughing so hard I couldn't breathe. I could feel my bladder starting to give way.

"Forty-one years," I thought. "It took forty-one years but he finally gave me something. The time of day!"

———

I pulled into my driveway just as my son Adam was parking his truck. It was a vintage Ford pickup. He'd had it for a week. I got it for him for his sixteenth birthday. As he hopped out of the truck, he said, "Hi, Dad," and hugged me. As I held my son in my arms, I realized how much time I had wasted thinking that I had missed out all those years. I hadn't. Not really. Sylvester had.

Afterword

Q. "What do you call a black man who flies airplanes?"
A. "A pilot, you fucking racist."

—a new twist on an old joke

It was a bright Saturday morning as I walked to the main branch of the San Leandro Community Library to do some background research for this book. The library is a majestic building, originally donated to the city by Andrew Carnegie himself, one of his many philanthropic atonements for a life lived as a robber baron. The library has recently been seismically retrofitted and updated with computers, audio/visual equipment, wireless technology, and all of the state-of-the-art contrivances that are expected to aid in the dissemination of information here in the twenty-first century. It is totally and thoroughly modern.

As I approached the front door, two little boys came bouncing out. One was black, the other white. They couldn't have been more than three or four years old. I watched as they laughed and giggled, playing together without a care in the world. I stopped and looked at them in wonder as they raced around the base of the library flagpole, Old Glory billowing proudly above in the wind. "Liberty and Justice for All."

A moment later, their respective mothers walked out behind them. Two women of different hues bound together by
the mutual backpacks of toys, children's books, and apple juice
boxes that they carried. Two moms just raising their kids and
watching them grow. No color chasm separated them. They
got no odd looks as library patrons walked past them going in
and out of the building. No one questioned their association or
the right of either family to be there. I watched in amazement
as I thought of how this city has changed and how proud I am
to have been a part of that change.

Not too long ago, when my daughter, Carolyn (who I'm
sure you know by now is named after Mom), was in the eighth
grade, one of her classmates called her a "nigger." It was a
white boy she'd known since kindergarten and it was the first
time she'd had that epithet used in reference to her. The funny
thing was that she was not upset by it. It was no big deal to
her. I, on the other hand, was apoplectic. I called Tracie at her
home in Sacramento.

"She's in the eighth grade?" Tracie asked.

"Yes."

"And this is the first time she's been called a 'nigger'?"

"Yes, Tracie. The first time."

"In San Leandro?"

"Yes, Tracie. In San Leandro."

"Wow!" she said. "Things really *are* better!"

She laughed, and I lost it right along with her. I hadn't put
it in that perspective. It took my daughter thirteen years to experience an indignity that I had faced after less than a week in
this town.

I marvel at the place that my children are growing up in today. San Leandro has gone from a place where whites desert
their churches because their pastor has the effrontery to engage

in fair-housing practices to a place where members of all races worship side by side in the pews of churches of all denominations. It has changed from a city that expected its police department to enforce de facto segregation, to the point of humiliating eight-year-old children for simply walking down the street or riding their bikes into town, to a city whose police department mentors children of all colors, teaching them about the dangers of associating with gangs and the scourge of illegal drug use. It has changed from a town with a real estate industry operating under subversive "gentlemen's agreements" not to show homes to people of certain complexions to a town whose Realtors value the diversity and contributions that all homeowners bring to the community.

As San Leandro has changed, I have changed as well. When all is said and done, I AM indeed a Genuine Black Man— because I am resilient. That's what being black in America is truly about: resilience. Our ancestors were kidnapped from their homes in Africa and brought across the ocean on slave ships. Most of them died during the journey. Only the resilient survived. Then our forefathers suffered four hundred years of bondage, followed by another century of legalized disenfranchisement. Again, only those who were resilient enough to persevere made it through. Had any of these people not had the fortitude to withstand the struggle, had they died as the result of it before starting families and planting the seeds of the future, my generation of African Americans would not exist. It is that resilience that enables my brethren to plant their own seeds for harvest in a better and brighter future.

I am as resilient as my forefathers. I have the fortitude of my mother and my grandmother. Even though I almost threw it away in a sad and sick moment, I am still here. I'm still standing. I stayed on my feet through taunts and harassment, through police intimidation and bigoted nuns, through school-yard bullies and Sylvester, through my mother's death and bouts of sometimes crippling depression. I am still standing.

I am black because, as my friend Mr. Wilkins once told me, people should be called what they *want* to be called. I have the right and the ability to determine my identity regardless of what other blacks *or* whites say. I am not an "oreo," nor am I "still a nigger." I am a man. I am a black man.

No one person or group of individuals holds the monopoly on what in this society is the "true" black experience. My world is as "black" as that of Malcolm X, Colin Powell, Snoop Dogg, Jesse Jackson, Usher, Bill Cosby, or Diddy. As their experiences in America are unique, mine is unique—yet it is the same. It is as valid as that of the poor African American living in "the 'hood," the rich black rapper balancing a lifestyle of fame and violence, and the black scholar working to better this world through academic dissertation. It is as authentic as the experiences of those who marched with Dr. King for civil rights and those who defy the black community by arguing the conservative point of view.

It is the "true" black experience because it is *my* experience. I defy anyone to say that it isn't as real, as joyous and as painful, as liberating and as confining, as frustrating and as exhilarating as that of any other similarly complected American. Black people in this country are not a monolith with one lifestyle, one viewpoint, and one agenda. The second that blacks or whites buy into that misguided belief is the very moment that all racial progress in this country has been negated.

In the end, I am grateful for that anonymous letter accusing me of not being a genuine black man, for it led me on a journey of self-exploration. If the letter writer is reading this, I thank you from the bottom of my heart.

I am grateful for encountering Judge James Ware at the time in my life that I did. In spite of his own apparent struggles with self-identity, I still admire him and I thank him for showing me by his very presence that within myself, I had the ability to be who and what I wanted to be. It took me a long time to figure that out. Especially in terms of my appearance. Once I finally did, I stopped straightening, Geri curling, "perming," and "relaxing" my hair. I love it because it's mine and it's just how God intended it to be.

People sometimes ask me if my mother made the right choice moving us to San Leandro, into that hostile environment. All I can say in response is, "It's my hometown."

I am proud and I am at peace. Genuinely.

Brian Copeland
San Leandro, California
July 2006

Resources

There are several resources that were invaluable in the researching of this book. To get a handle on the political situation and machinations that allowed San Leandro to segregate its community, I consulted Robert O. Self's book *American Babylon: Race and the Struggle for Post War Oakland* and Self's essay "Black Power City, White Power Suburb."

San Leandro resident Don Magnifico wrote a term paper for a Cal State Hayward sociology class in 1969 that detailed the power of San Leandro's ten homeowner's associations in keeping the city all white. This work provided me with several quotes from contemporary residents.

For San Leandro's beginnings, Cindy Simons of the San Leandro Library provided me with her essay, "A History of San Leandro."

Filmmaker Paul Altmyer's 1971 documentary, *The Suburban Wall*, allowed me to actually hear the rationalizations for keeping blacks out of San Leandro from the mouths of the city fathers themselves. It provided crucial context.

Several periodicals were also of great use including *Newsweek, The Morning News, The Call Bulletin, The Hayward Daily Review* and the *San Francisco Chronicle*. It is the *Chronicle's* archives that follow and detail the revelations of the James Ware/Virgil Ware story.

The records of San Leandro Fair Housing were of tremendous value in getting a feel for what the advocates of an open housing policy were up against in the early '70s.

Finally, the generosity of Mel and Doris Desoto, Glennie Noste and Mimi Wilson in taking the time to submit to numerous interviews with their recollections of the fair housing fight had an immeasurable impact on this work.

Acknowledgments

There are many, many people who have been instrumental in the inspiration, researching, and writing of this book.

First and foremost, I want to thank my mother, Carolyn Copeland, and my grandmother, Lena Arbee. Without your love, guidance, and strength, not only wouldn't there be a book and a play, there wouldn't be a Brian.

Thanks to my sister Tracie Copeland Stafford for her love, friendship, and support and for always having my back.

I thank my sisters Delisa Copeland Brock, Tonya Copeland, and Heather Copeland for their encouragement and love.

I want to thank my wonderful wife, Susan Taylor Copeland, for telling me that I could write this story, even when I didn't believe it myself. Thanks for being there for me during the hard days. Most importantly, thanks for coming up with the funniest line in the show.

Thanks to David Ford for listening to my kooky idea about a show on housing discrimination and suicidal depression and helping me transform it into something I've always wanted (and needed) to say.

Stephanie Weisman at The Marsh for giving the idea a chance to blossom on her stage.

Diana Rathbone, Dot Jansen, and Johnathann Meier at The Marsh for all of your kindness and encouragement.

David Hines for holding my hand through every performance of this story.

Penny Peck and Cindy Simons of the San Leandro Public Library for their help in researching the history of San Leandro and its discriminatory policies.

Don Magnifico for the gracious use of his 1969 term paper on housing discrimination in San Leandro.

Mimi Wilson, Mel and Doris Desoto, Glennie Noste, and the other brave souls who fought harassment and intimidation to start San Leandro Fair Housing in the '60s and '70s.

Beth Wilcoxin for her kindness, encouragement, and her remembrances of her father, Reverend Dorel Londagin, a true hero.

Jan and the gang at Sabino's for their encouragement as I wrote this thing at my usual corner table.

My literary agent, Amy Rennert, for her guidance and faith in this project.

My editors at Hyperion, Kelly Notaras and Ruth Curry.

Bob and Linda Taylor and John and Barbara Taylor for their love and support.

Norm Arslan for helping me through the fog that enabled me to tell this story.

Jonnie Jacobs and Camille Minichino for believing I was a real writer when I was scared to death of the blank page.

My brothers from other mothers, Jon Regan, Mark Lyell, and "Chicago" Steve Barkley.

Joe and Judy Galvan, just 'cause.

My distinguished colleagues at KGO Radio in San Francisco, especially Ronn Owens and Gene Burns for their help in bringing both versions of this work to the world.

And last, but certainly not least, the legendary Carl Reiner for helping me to find my very own piece of ground.